INSIDE THE MIND OF

JEFFREY DAHMER

THE CANNIBAL KILLER

CHRISTOPHER BERRY-DEE

First published in 2022 by Ad Lib Publishers Ltd
15 Church Road
London, SW13 9HE

www.adlibpublishers.com

Text © 2022 Christopher Berry-Dee

ISBN 9781913543310
eBook ISBN 9781802470000

A CIP catalogue record for this book is available from the British Library.

Every reasonable effort has been made to trace copyright-holders of material reproduced in this book, but if any have been inadvertently overlooked the publishers would be glad to hear from them.

Printed in the UK
10 9 8 7 6 5 4 3 2 1

INSIDE THE MIND OF
JEFFREY DAHMER

For HM Royal Marines Commando WOII Mark Hayes; his wife Sam; all past, present and future Royal Marines who ascribe to earn the coveted Green Beret. We are family and *always* will be.

Contents

Prologue   11

Introduction   15

Inside the Mind of Jeffrey Dahmer   21

Dahmer's Formative Years   36

Whittier School, Ames   54

Hazel Elementary School, Barberton   61

Eastview Junior High School   68

Revere High School   75

Divorce   92

Crossing the Rubicon – Steven Mark Hicks   99

Mind Control   107

Medical Specialist in the Army   112

The 'Last Chance Saloon'   120

Stephen 'Steve' Walter Tuomi 127

James 'Jamie' Edward Doxator 134

Richard Guerrero 137

Corpse Love 139

Keison Sinthasomphone 143

Anthony Lee Sears 145

Raymond Lamont Smith 148

Edward 'Eddie' Warren Smith 153

Ernest Marquez Miller 155

David Courtney Thomas 157

Curtis Durrell Straughter 159

Errol Scott Lindsey 161

Anthony 'Tony' Hughes 163

Stinking to High Heaven 164

Konerak Sinthasomphone 166

Matt Cleveland Turner 172

Jeremiah B. Weinberger 174

Oliver Joseph Lacy 176

Joseph Bradehoft 179

Tracy Edwards 184

The Abattoir 193

Enter the Psychiatrists   203

Just Penance   220

In conclusion: what made Jeffrey Dahmer?   224

Appendix   233

Notes   255

Prologue

'For what judgment ye judge, ye shall be judged. For whatever judgment you judge, you will be judged; and with whatever measure you measure, it will be measured to you.'

Matthew 7:2

In approaching the indelicate subject of Jeffrey Dahmer as we do now, we might bring to the debating table our own individual preconceived thoughts, judgements and biases, so as to measure what sort of person Jeffrey was. One is certainly *not* wrong in considering him to be an unrepentant, cold-blooded, sado-sexual, psychopathic monster through and through. For my part I dare imagine that, if it had been *my* young son who had fallen prey to his necrophiliac, cannibalistic predations – had a hole drilled into his skull while he was semi-drugged, and then had acid or boiling water poured into his brain in an effort to turn him into a compliant sex zombie – I would have wanted to inflict upon Mr Dahmer the most extreme and tortuous death. As a former HM Royal

Marines 'Green Beret' Commando, I would have been Hell-bent on retribution. I would have taken Jeremiah 31:34: 'For I forgive their wickedness and will remember their sins no more' and flung it into the abyss. I would have been unable to contemplate Luke 23:24: 'Father, forgive them, for they know not what they are doing'. I would have been unable to forgive or to contemplate any investigation into why a man would do this to another human being.

In today's more 'enlightened' society (can I say so far Leftie society?) there are those who hold more compassionate feelings towards those who are 'fallen from grace'. Perhaps they are people of more devoted Christian leanings than myself – that is until one of their own young kith and kin is butchered by a man such as Jeffrey Dahmer. Were they to experience such a tragedy, it would be as if they have seen the 'true light' shining upon them. They would upend their pulpit-bashing rhetoric, and return, forthwith, back down to planet Earth... with a bang! I know that there will be countless critics out there who will say that I am heartless and without soul. My literary style can be controversial, but I believe that one can't make an omelette without breaking some eggs.

There might those who might say that while the 'Milwaukee Cannibal' didn't deserve to be executed because of his human rights, he did get his just deserts in the unique and brutal manner of his death. This book is not about whether Dahmer's punishment was true justice. It is about what made this man-monster tick. What I want to do is put Dahmer under a glass so that we can study him as one might dispassionately and microscopically examine a blowfly preserved in amber. In fact this is *precisely* what Dahmer did to insects and small animals from an early age. His early destruction of small creatures escalated to the destruction of innocent young men. He developed his pseudo post-mortem skills on drugged, still living human beings, inflicting upon them – like some deranged Nazi concentration-camp doctor – the most God-awful, terrible medical experiments. Why do we need to study someone as abhorrent as Dahmer? Because experience tells us that one of these real life, human flesh-eating nightmares – like something from a Stephen King novel – became all too real in Milwaukee, USA.

So, this book comes with a mental health warning. Although much has already been written and documented about Dahmer, I ask the reader to come along with me with a cool head. I ask you to measure and to judge Dahmer for yourself. In this book we will literally try to dissect Dahmer's psychopathology, throughout the genesis of his murderous career. I might get some of this study right and I might get some of it wrong (critics, please note). I want to try and answer a bald question often put to me at lectures and in correspondence from my readers: What makes killers like Dahmer tick?

With some serial killers, we really do not have even a solid clue what makes them do the terrible things they do because there is scant evidence that we can totally rely upon. With Dahmer, however, there is a treasure trove to be unearthed. His history is well documented from cradle to grave. Most of the killers I have interviewed possess no inkling as to what negative influences propelled them down the road to committing serial homicide most foul. In this respect, Dahmer himself offers us few of the answers. Or does he? Perhaps his parents will also have an insight into the origins of the murderer their son became. It can be tempting to want to dismiss and forget someone as violent as Dahmer, but it will become apparent that nurture played a very large, almost tear-jerking part in Dahmer's early years. By addressing the very darkest corners of serial killer history we can learn much about the nature of humanity. Perhaps, if you are a good loving parent or someone with at least a level of compassion, you may view Dahmer in a totally different light altogether... or maybe not.

Try not to have nightmares.

Introduction

> '*He who fights with monsters might take care lest he thereby become a monster. And if you gaze for long into an abyss, the abyss gazes also into you.*'
>
> Friedrich Nietzsche (1844-1900)

Aside from Theodore 'Ted' Robert Bundy (1946-1989), cannibal and necrophile Jeffrey Lionel Dahmer (1960-1995) is amongst the most documented serial killers in criminal history. His crimes have been reported in countless newspaper and magazine articles and recounted in numerous documentaries and films. Even twenty-seven years after his death, psychiatrists and psychologists still bicker over his state of mind, even getting into legal proceedings and bunfights when things get overheated. 'So, why another book on Jeffrey Dahmer?' is a question you might rightly ask. 'So, what more is there to learn, Christopher?' To answer some of this we must start at the beginning.

The origin of the name 'Jeffrey' is Germanic, meaning 'God's peace (*Gottes frieden*)' or 'divine peace (*göttlicher frieden*)', which, in Jeffrey's case seems misapplied. During my career, I have interviewed face-to-face and studied some thirty serial killers, mass murderers and one-off wanton takers of human life. I *almost* met Jeffrey Dahmer. I got side-tracked, you see. Instead of meeting with Dahmer, I was interviewing nursing aide Gwendolyn Gail Graham for a twelve-part TV series called *The Serial Killers*.

Graham was one half of the killing tag team that the media dubbed the 'Lethal Lovers'. She and Cathy May Wood, during the ice-cold winter of 1987, enjoyed a sickening love pact. They suffocated – by kneeling on their chests, pinching their noses and forcing their hands over dry mouths and pursed lips – five elderly residents of the Alpine Manor nursing home in the Walker suburb of Grand Rapids, Michigan. I eventually interviewed both of these monsters. The scrawny Graham at the Women's Huron Valley Correctional Facility, Michigan, and the grossly obese Wood, then incarcerated in the Federal Correctional Institution, Tallahassee, Florida. Cathy Wood was released from prison on 16 January 2020. Graham will only be freed wearing a cardboard coffin.

We had already filmed a programme about William 'Bill' Heirens aka 'The Lipstick Killer' in the 'windy city'. I interviewed Bill at the Dixon Correctional Center, in Dixon County, Illinois. We had also made a John Wayne Gacy documentary in Chicago. Finding ourselves in the 'Great Lakes State' of Michigan, it was a toss-up between interviewing Jeffrey Dahmer or Gwendolyn Graham.

We'd already interviewed Cathy Wood in California so my producer, Frazer Ashford – with his beady eye on the production budget – decided that Gwendolyn would make a double whammy for a single programme. Two for the price of one. So, Dahmer was off the menu, period!

Despite Dahmer not being on the roster of murderers I have had the dubious privilege of speaking with directly, in this book I'd like to try and delve much deeper into his psychopathology than previously attempted by other writers, psychologists and psychiatrists. A study of the deepest recesses of someone like Dahmer's mind should be of equal interest to us criminologists as his heinous crimes. I also firmly believe that *if* we are to understand what makes *any* serial killer tick the answer is, more often than not, sitting in plain sight. If one can tune into the right wavelength the answers are logical even as they are dark.

As all of my loyal readers around the world already know, I am one for being matter-of-fact, up-front and saying it as it is with no BS involved. More importantly, I emphasise giving the deepest respect for the victims and their grieving next of kin. However, at times, I flip the coin over and inject some black humour to add a seasoning of ungracious levity to my work. I might also drift from the given path into trivia as is my wont, just to lighten the load on these very heavy stories I am telling.

I also attempt to use easy to understand analogies. While the 'shrinks' might inadvertently confuse us with psychobabble I prefer to use more simple terms that my readers can both understand and gain insight from. This is not to say that I always have the right approach and they do not – but many of the experts in their fields have a habit of talking *at* us rather than *with* us. There is big difference in my approach to these matters. When I am trying to sift through highly professional papers and extract what I believe is the essence of the argument to my readers, I always look for ways to highlight particular issues and direct them to study it further elsewhere as it pleases them. I enjoy bringing my readers along with me on my literary road trips – let's call them 'psycho travelogues' – into the evilest of mindsets. I want my readers to explore along with me so that they, too, get up close and personal with monsters. This stuff can damage one's mind and this book is not for the squeamish, nor suitable for a bedtime read. So soon enough we will be turning the dial to tune into the right wavelength and the Dahmer programme, so to speak.

*

'I have been assured by a very knowing American of my acquaintance in London, that a young healthy child well-nursed is at a year old a most delicious, nourishing, and wholesome food, whether stewed, roasted, baked, or boiled; and I make no doubt that it will equally serve in a fricassee or a ragout.'

Jonathan Swift (1667-1745)

The killer Arthur John Shawcross (1945-2008) who, in his first ever TV interview filmed on 19 September 1994 at the Sullivan Correctional Facility, Fallsburg, New York, told me with more than a modicum of culinary hyperbole:

'I have been asked, did I kill? Yes, too many times for any one person to do so! It is said I have partaken of human flesh. Think back in history. You will see that man hunted man (still do in some remote parts of the world). Think about the animal we call pig or boar. Why does it say in some books we can't eat this animal? Because it tastes just like human flesh.

I have eaten flesh of man or woman. So, the next time any of you sit down to eat bacon, ham or a nice juicy pot roast or pork chop, think about the taste, the flavour of eating human flesh.

I like my meat raw. Bleeding. Any meat I eat raw. But this only affected me when I got very angry – the hunger of a predator.

Oh, by the way, would you be the best man at my wedding to my beloved Clara [his fiancée]?'

'Art' didn't mince his words. Shawcross liked to brag that he'd killed and butchered several Vietnamese lasses then eaten parts of them on his 'special missions' whilst he served with the US army during the Vietnam war. In truth, Shawcross aka 'The Monster of the Rivers' was merely an armoury clerk in Vietnam. He never came within a hundred kilometres of a red-hot bullet, but he did go on to kill thirteen more women including two children. And Shawcross did partly eat a single piece of human flesh from one of them. So, close your eyes now, and hear the dreadful truth. Having murdered and dumped thirty-four-year-old sex worker, June Cicero, 'Art' returned to her frozen body later and hacked out her vagina. He thawed this human organ under his car's heater. At interview he said to me and my wide-eyed film crew – staring at us with his ever-blinking, porcine eyes – 'I just chewed some flesh off, and um, throwed it away. Then I went down to a Dunkin' Donuts stall for coffee and talked to the dumb fuckin' cops to find out who the serial killer could be they were looking for.' 'Art' also wrote *The Cannibal Cookbook*, and I have the only copy of his indigestible manuscript. For reasons that I cannot explain, I have not yet tried any of the recipes.

So I am not unfamiliar with the horrors of murderers who go on to violate the corpses of their victims. And yet – and please s'cuse the totally un-called-for unintended pun – it has to be said that Dahmer – also known as the Milwaukee Cannibal – often went the whole hog in this respect. And Dahmer's desire to consume the flesh of his victims is perhaps what makes Dahmer such a fascinating and abhorrent figure in the True Crime world. Now, before we start, does anyone fancy a take-out kebab?

Christopher Berry-Dee
Hampshire, UK & El Nido, Palawan, Philippines
www.christopherberrydee.com

Inside the Mind of Jeffrey Dahmer

'I froze some of the meat to eat at my own convenience.'

Jeffrey Dahmer

I always prefer to begin my books on a soft note – one that doesn't cause immediate alarm, most especially to the reader who has a delicate disposition. It's unlikely that anyone is reading this book with no knowledge at all of what Dahmer was. But perhaps an older lady – a grandma maybe – may have picked this tome up. Perhaps a softly spoken grandma who likes things neat and tidy and spick and span. I think they might even like Jeffrey, at first glance, because his one-bedroom apartment in Milwaukee was by all accounts for a bachelor, kept quite tidy. But there is little point in beating around the bush when it comes to Jeffrey Dahmer. So, to quote the famous fictional cannibal killer, Hannibal Lector: *'Bowels in or bowels out?'[1]*

Making no bones about it, Jeffrey Dahmer killed seventeen young men. We will come to learn who these unfortunates were; when, where, and how they were killed; what Dahmer did to these victims prior to their deaths and post-mortem. But first, let's indulge in some of the relevant trivia I promised earlier.

Depending upon which source one consults, blood volume varies by gender and weight. If you are the average adult you will have between nine and twelve pints of blood in your body. An average-sized woman has about nine pints (5.1 litres) and the average-sized man about twelve pints (6.8 litres). Scientists estimate that the volume of blood in the 'Average Joe' is approximately seven per cent of body weight. To further pique your interest, twelve pints of blood would easily cover fifty square feet. Using this information, we can estimate how much blood loss Dahmer caused while killing and butchering his victims. Seventeen victims with around twelve pints each means that Dahmer spilled 204 pints (115.9 litres) of his victims' blood, give or take a few extra drops, drips and splashes here and there.

Platelets, or thrombocytes, are inestimably small colourless cell fragments contained in our blood. We might not even give them a moment of thought, but they form clots – so when one pricks one's finger, they gang up and rush to the injury site as if some urgent clarion call has been sounded in our bone marrow and they stop you from bleeding to death. That's where platelets are made you see – in your marrow. A normal platelet count in the 'Average Joe' ranges from 150,000 to 450,000 platelets per microlitre of blood. At this point you might need to seek out someone who is into infinitesimal calculus – someone who spends their days writing lots of unintelligible symbols on a blackboard then rubbing it all off again – because a microlitre is a unit of volume equal to one millionth of a litre. If one were to spread all of Jeff's seventeen victims' platelets out they would cover an area roughly the size of Uzbekistan, perhaps with enough left over to paint the Golden Gate Bridge – twice. So, Jeffrey Dahmer spilled a terrific amount of blood during his murderous career.

There are, of course, other bodily fluids as well as organs that will need consideration when it comes to dismemberment of a body. Don Davis writes with obvious relish in his book *The Jeffrey Dahmer Story: An American Nightmare*: 'Once the heart stops beating about four times per breath, it becomes just a lump – as big as fist and weighing just under a pound. Then there is the stomach, that J-shaped receptacle that takes up space in the middle of the torso, up to thirty feet of intestine, and a brain weighing about three mushy pounds.'[2] Our Don's got a way with words, hasn't he? Don goes on to explain that it isn't easy to dispose of a human corpse. There are 656 muscles in the human form, and some are more than a foot in length. Although they are relatively soft, they are fibrous and strong and can resist even the sharpest knife.

Don also ruminates on the number of bones in the human body – 206 in total – a multitude of big and little obstacles to the saw. Each arm contains thirty-two bones, and each leg contains thirty-one. The skull is not one single bone but is actually made up of twenty-nine different bones. The spine is made up of twenty-six. There are six in each ear, and even two in the throat – the hyoid and the clavicle. The hardest bones within the human body are the teeth and there are about thirty-two of them in the 'Average Joe'

– unless one has been a prize-fighter or my own grandma, who kept her teeth in a glass of water by her bed.

To be honest with you, I have never met Don Davis, but from reading his book I can tell he's my kinda guy. I'm obliged to point out that in his summary of the workings of the human body he singly failed to mention that the 'Average Joe's' body also contains up to 100,000 miles of blood vessels and all the arteries, veins, and capillaries which, if stretched end-to-end, would wrap around the Earth more than twice. Multiply that by seventeen victims and you have 1,700,000 miles: enough to circle the planet forty-two-and-a-half times. Yep, in total: 510 feet of intestine; 11,152 feet of muscle material; 3,150 assorted bones; 493 sundry parts of skull and 442 bits of spine. Can you even begin to imagine how one might manage to clean up that amount of mess then dispose of it? It surely beats the hell out of me. However, we will not for long be left in the dark, because Jeffrey Dahmer will tell how it was all done in the chapters to follow.

For most of us, it's inherently human to recoil at the notion of death and the human corpse but the human brain is the most complicated machine that has ever existed, or will ever exist, if the truth be told. And the human mind is a wondrous thing which we will never fully understand because its very essence is beautifully magical. The human mind constantly processes new bits and pieces of information. It is forever evolving, always learning, always forgetting and always ever dying. Yet inside some human minds there sits evil: a wickedness so dark that therein lies the abyss.

Serial killer, John Reginald Halliday Christie admitted to having a cup of tea with the corpse of one of his victims, Rita Nelson, before he disposed of her body. He was quoted as saying: 'Having a cup of tea seems as much a part of my murder career as whisky is with other murderers. For me a corpse has a beauty and dignity, which a living body could never hold. There is a peace about death that soothes me.' When we come to reflect on Dahmer's crimes, we might conceive that he could have taken those few lines, plucked from Christie's homicidal narrative, and implanted them in his own life story.

During my lengthy career as an investigative criminologist I have spent thousands of hours researching the lives and the crimes of sexually motivated murderers. Without wishing to come across as stating the obvious, or becoming overtly philosophical, I have arrived at a conclusion: that every life – like every book, painting, poem or design – starts with a blank page. In fact *you* started your very own existence as a blank page – the only invisible marks on it being your ancestral DNA, which in itself, is something we are only recently starting to understand. Hey, and guess what: when scientists mapped the genetics of frogs and humans they found that their genes have very similar patterns about ninety per cent of the time. In other words, the frog genome contains the same sort of 'gene neighbourhoods' as the human genome. So it seems to me that it's a pure fluke that instead of sitting at my desk writing this book I could have been wearing a slimy green suit and sitting on a waterlily leaf in the middle of a duck pond!

'Don't judge each day by the harvest you reap
but by the seeds you plant.'

Robert Louis Stevenson (1850-1894)

Internationally respected psychoanalyst, Dr Alice Miller, in her bestselling book, *The Drama of the Gifted Child*[3] compared new human life to an acorn that grows into an oak tree. The way the tree grows is affected by its surroundings, the weather and the environment. It could grow into a beautiful, strong tree but if the environment allows it could grow into something warped and gnarled.

Let's think about Dr Miller's words for a moment or two as we begin to digest, in bite-sized chunks, Jeffrey Dahmer's life from cradle to grave. Here we are, at the start of our psycho-travelogue into DahmerLand. A life that began as we all do, with a blank page but terminated in ashes to ashes and dust to dust and an unfathomable amount of bloodshed. For, like all of us, Dahmer emerged from his mother's womb a helpless and innocent baby that needed nurturing as do we all. And yet, did he develop in a healthy way to become a human being, who would become useful and valued by society? No, he did not. We can speculate as to whether Jeff Dahmer's life started with a first-rate double helix – the structure formed by double-stranded molecules of nucleic acids such as DNA – a genetically clean page with no known defects that might influence his life choices. Or perhaps it was later, once he was able to take in his surroundings that things happened. Perhaps it was the manner in which he was treated by his parents during his impressionable formative years. What genetic or external social influences influenced him and what psychological processes came into play? Was there a bad genetic seed? Was it the way he was raised? Are we looking at a case of nature *or* nurture, or a combination of nature *and* nurture? How was it that this young man from an apparently good home and normal, everyday parents metamorphosed into something that would become the stuff of our worst nightmares – a nocturnal, flesh-eating beast? Was Jeffrey Lionel Dahmer the work of the Devil?

But wait, because Dr Alice Miller argued that *all* parents are unwittingly cruel to their offspring and not just through overt abuse and violence but through smaller instances of humiliation, neglect and lack of attention. 'Miller's views may be extreme,' wrote Matt Seaton in *The Guardian* in 2005,[4] 'but they are hugely influential, challenging, controversial but impossible to ignore.' Dr Miller's book sent an entire generation of adults scurrying into therapy – much to the delight of American therapists – who I think amount to one in ten of the U.S. population. Miller went further to argue that children protect their parents from the truth about their parenting failures – always striving to earn their approval and even idealising their care-givers into adulthood. And the interesting thing is that Jeffrey Dahmer did just that. Apart from the odd occasion when he became upset over something, Dahmer never said a bad word against his mother or his father.

Matt Seaton says, 'Dr Miller's model of family relationships has become a landmark for everyone from child abuse professionals to the self-helping public. More than anything else, Miller put people in touch with their 'inner child', encouraging them to own 'their own truth'. Arguably, by this, Miller meant 'the truth of their own abuse', which, in essence requires one to psychoanalyse oneself.

Personally, I think that this self-help malarkey and self-help books, pamphlets, internet sites and forums are all tickety-boo if one wishes to fix a new fan belt on a 1960s Ford Anglia or learn how to darn one's socks without impaling one's finger and getting septicaemia because your platelets are on vacation. I get that much, but did you know that one can find self-help books online that advise us on which self-help books to choose? Reading self-help books to put you in touch with your own self is a 'no!' says I.

What would have happened if Dr Miller had suggested that psychopathic Jeff Dahmer put himself in touch with his inner child? Can one imagine asking a schizophrenic or someone with a similar underlying condition to start analysing him or herself? They have institutions employing psychiatrists for that very purpose, do they not? Maybe our mental health institutions are not perfect. Sometimes even the head investigators are not always up to scratch themselves.

I recall the hospital psychiatrists, Dr Udwin and Dr McGrath, freeing the arch-poisoner Graham Young from Broadmoor, claiming that: 'This man [Young] has suffered a deep-going personality disorder throughout most of his adolescence. He has, however, made an extremely full recovery and is now entirely fit for discharge, his sole disability now being the need to catch up on lost time.' How they came to this conclusion is baffling, for Young spent his time in Broadmoor wandering around performing

Nazi salutes, wearing a swastika around his neck, sporting a clipped Adolf moustache and telling all who would lend him an ear that 'The Final Solution' was no bad thing – the latter completely going over the head of Dr Udwin who was himself Jewish. But, yes, upon release Graham Young most certainly did 'catch up on lost time'. For even while still held in Broadmoor, he was poisoning staff and other patients' tea with belladonna that he extracted from laurel leaves or toilet bleach. And within a week of starting work as a storeman at a company specialising in cameras and optical equipment, he was poisoning his workmates, two of whom died and others going on to suffer agonies for the remainder of their days.

It's generally accepted that a child raised in a healthy home environment, enjoying a good diet, stable schooling, with law-abiding and loving parents, is most likely to grow up to become a decent, hardworking adult in their parents' image. It's what we might call 'positive parental conditioning'. There are exceptions of course: Kim Philby the British spy, who turned traitor to spy for the USSR during World War II and the start of the Cold War, came from a loving home and became one of the infamous 'Cambridge Spy Ring'. So if you want to become a spy the University of Cambridge might be a starter for ten. However, abuse of children – be it physical or psychological – can take many forms. It is not so much the nature of the maltreatment as it is about *how* the child perceives it and *how* it impacts on the child's developing mind. And, indeed, a child may look like they come from what may appear to others to be a healthy home, but it is what actually goes on behind closed doors, curtained windows and remains hidden from view which should concern us. And indeed it should concern us with regard to Jeffrey Dahmer, who did, it seems, come from a good home.

Sadly, many other children have their formative years built on shifting foundations. They have endured troublesome childhoods; abusive or violent parents; an absent or overbearing father or mother; parents whose relationships are strained and even violent; even an acrimonious divorce might impact on the youngster's personality. The child could witness substance abuse; be subjected to disruptive schooling; have an unsettled home life and poor diet. All of these things can seriously damage the developing mind, and possibly sow the seeds for what the child grows to perceive as 'normal behaviour' and then goes on to re-enact in the decades to follow. We could be so bold as to suggest that this would be termed 'negative parental conditioning'. Disrupted childhoods can lead to delinquency, an early criminal record and, as ever more lenient prison terms are handed out, this unchecked antisocial behaviour will inevitably lead to an ever-growing spiral of criminal activity, all of which negatively impacts on society as a whole. Do we not see this year-in year-out in our societies today? Feral youths running amok at night, showing no respect to decent, law-abiding citizens and even less deference for police, law and order? Of course we do. As I mentioned earlier, one does not need a degree in any of the social sciences to figure any of this out.

The renowned Canadian social anthropologist and author, Professor Elliott Leyton, is amongst the most widely consulted experts on serial homicide worldwide. Like Dr

Alice Miller, Elliott is something of a renegade amongst his peers and known for being outspoken. I paraphrase from a correspondence we shared: 'Christopher, millions of kids grow up in dysfunctional environments, but they do not all become serial killers, *do they*?' I'm inclined to agree with him: many individuals survive appallingly abusive and neglected childhoods and become decent, moral and honest adults. Professor Leyton is stating the obvious. However, it is also correct to note that the FBI carried out studies into criminal profiling during the 1970s and 1980s. Agent John Douglas, now immortalised by the TV series *Mindhunter*, interviewed dozens of incarcerated serial killers and used them to create a strategy for identifying, capturing and predicting the movements of serial predators. Douglas's work came to the conclusion that a dysfunctional childhood played *some part* in the majority of the developing antisocial narratives in most of the interview subjects.

One of the FBI's predictors for a young child developing a serious antisocial personality as they mature is the way they are treated by their parents during their formative years, for during this precious time a child's brain soaks up information like a sponge. And it is here that Dr Miller's work intersects when we examine Jeff's early years. It is during these early years that everything that is going on around the child *will* form the basis – the psychological foundations – for all that is to come. This is an issue of much import as we examine Jeffrey Dahmer in more depth.

I like to look at this with a 'layer cake' perspective. Day-after-day, week-after-week, month-in month-out, a child from a dysfunctional background is subjected to layer upon layer of varying forms of psychological and physical abuse until he or she begins to accept this behaviour and maltreatment as the norm. As Dr Miller rightly concludes, the child is not in a position to correct its parents, and so the child becomes numbed to their reality. Therefore, eventually the child accepts it and it becomes irrevocably ingrained in the preteen's pathology. I find this particularly applicable in young children who metamorphose into criminals because most youngsters are simply *not* in the position to question or critically examine their parents or their teachers even when the adults are patently wrong. The young child learns from, and is taught by, its elders. The Latin word *docere* means 'to teach' and is the root of the word 'indoctrinate'. Originally, this is *exactly* what it meant. By setting a good example, parents are giving their children a type of behaviour that they can emulate within their own life. Dahmer's parents did exactly the opposite.

When an airplane navigates through the sky it works its way along a route composed of beacons and waypoints – invisible signposts in the sky – which are defined by geographic coordinates. They constitute the pilot's map of the world. Flight computers are programmed into these waypoints which are put into the systems before take-off. Assuming these coordinates have been programmed correctly, the plane will go from point A, passing through the designated waypoints, before arriving at point B without a hitch. However, if any of these waypoints are wrong, the aircraft will deviate from its flight programme and its destination which can prove fatal. Life for each of us contains thousands of waypoints; signposts that hopefully provide us with directions as to what to do, how to go about things and where to go next – our decision-making processes. But what happens when our own onboard computer, our brain, has initially been programmed with data that is corrupt and socially unacceptable. How are we able to make to make life decisions – correct decisions that is?

The child who has been negatively wired up is easily capable of making the wrong decisions; make asocial decisions and going to the wrong places in their adult life because there is every probability that he or she knows no better. The child who has been socially programmed in a positive manner is far better mentally-equipped to make the correct moral and social decisions and go to more healthy and safe places. The conditioning of a child is akin to giving them a good set of waypoints. And we must consider the waypoints that were given to Dahmer and that guided his trajectory, if we are to try to get inside of his head. Did the 'Milwaukee Cannibal', like so many of his murderous breed, suffer from a dysfunctional childhood? Jeffrey Dahmer has admitted that he himself didn't know the answer when he said in his flat-as-a-pancake monotone voice: 'I am what I am. I don't even know what I am or why I am. But I did what I did, and I don't even know how to say sorry.'

We know from many case studies that the father figure is one of the major factors determining the character of the child during infancy, particularly when it comes to boys. In cases where the father is a fairly well-integrated individual and presents a consistent pattern of behaviour which the small boy can respect, he becomes a role model which the child strives to emulate. The image the child has of his father becomes the cornerstone of his later character, so that he is able to integrate his own behaviour along socially accepted lines. The importance of this first step in character development cannot be overestimated. It is almost a pre-requisite for a stable, secure and well-integrated personality in later life. In all of this, Jeff's father, Lionel, ruefully admits he is lacking.

As for the mother's role as primary caretaker? It is known that boys who share a healthy relationship with their mothers from their early childhood are emotionally strong and are believed to have less behavioural problems in their lives. The strong bond between mother and son makes him feel secure and confident. Studies indicate that boys who do not have a healthy bond with their mothers in early childhood could be hostile and aggressive in their later years, or insecure in relationships and establishing goals. A study published in the August 2011 edition of *Child Development* says that: '… the unconditional love and acceptance of the mother reassures the son that he is lovable and capable of being a good friend and lover.' The study also reveals that the more loving a mother, the fewer are the chances of the boy being distant and cold. So as we start to examine Jeff Dahmer's life we must understand that the bond between mother and baby begins right inside her womb. The son picks up his first emotions from the mother and, as the nurturing continues, he should grow up to be emotionally intelligent and strong. Research also indicated that good mother-son bonding will ensure lower levels of psychological distress in children. When his needs are being taken care of by his mother, he learns to trust and feel emotional security. In all of this, Jeff's mother, Joyce, maintains that she was the perfect mum, which, as will soon become obvious, she was anything but.

Dahmer's Formative Years

'I think we are fascinated by Dahmer's childhood because it was a more normal childhood. He wasn't in reform school. He wasn't arrested as a kid. He had a family around him. He had parents, a younger brother. He had a nice home. How could someone possibly do the things he did given his background. He had everything going for him. What happened?'

Dr Mike Kukral, Dahmer's long-time friend at Revere High School, speaking on the TV documentary *Jeffrey Dahmer: Mind of a Monster*

Jeffrey Lionel Dahmer was born at 4.34 p.m., weighing six pounds and fifteen ounces, on 21 May 1960, at the Evangelical Deaconess Hospital, Milwaukee, in the 'Badger State', Wisconsin. He was the first of two sons, with David following in 1966. As author Brian Masters writes in *The Shrine of Jeffrey Dahmer*:[5] 'The couple [Joyce and Lionel Dahmer] were entranced with their auburn-haired, luminously blue-eyed baby ... their life *momentarily* [my italics] joyous as a result as a subtle portent of things to come.' Lionel Herbert Dahmer was an engineering student at Marquette University, Wisconsin Avenue, in downtown

Milwaukee at the time of his first son's birth. The name 'Dahmer' is North German/ Danish: the habitational name for someone from any of various places called Dahme, in Holstein, Mecklenburg, Brandenburg, or Silesia. Lionel's father and his family had emigrated from Germany in the nineteenth century. His mother, Catherine Hughes, was of Welsh descent.

Of Norwegian/Irish descent and several months older than her husband, his wife was a teletype machine instructor. Joyce Annette Flint was born on 7 February 1936. Her parents were Floyd 'Rocky' Flint and Lillian B. Flint née Rundberg. The surname actually has Scandinavian roots which is not unexpected considering that Schleswig-Holstein shares its Northern borders with Denmark. She would claim that her father was a brutal alcoholic and spent little to no time with her, thus she craved attention.

At first, they lived in the downstairs flat of Lionel's mother's home in the quiet suburban community of West Allis. Joyce had fallen pregnant within days of them tying the knot, and her pregnancy was difficult. Already prone to mood swings, these increased. She wanted more attention from Lionel, whom she thought was more married to his work than to her. She started to sulk and spent pretty much the whole of February and March 1960 in bed with all manner of ills, eventually having to give up work – which made her even more irritated.

On Joyce's pregnancy with Jeffrey, Lionel Dahmer recalled:

> 'During her pregnancy, Joyce developed seizure-
> type symptoms and the doctors would prescribe

her barbiturates to calm her down because her body would become rigid, and she would develop a little bit of foam in the mouth. Unfortunately the doctors didn't discover what it was. She was taking twenty-seven pills a day while she was pregnant including antidepressants, progesterone, and growth hormones. Her jaw would go sideways and lock. Her eyes would bulge, which sort of sounds like epilepsy, a seizure of some type but the doctor did not say that was what it was. He just didn't know what it was. The doctor often had to intervene giving her injections of barbiturates and morphine, which would finally relax her.'

Joyce ended up being prescribed drugs to help her through the pregnancy. Lionel Dahmer later questioned whether or not the drugs his wife was taking had affected the baby. Later, as he spiralled into endless second-guessing about the upbringing of Jeff, there is one last agonising possibility that still haunts him. He explained in a TV interview in April 2017, that the drugs prescribed to his wife when she was pregnant might have harmed the foetus.

Those of more sympathetic leanings than myself are right when they say that there can be no doubt that Joyce was rendered ill by her pregnancy. But her behaviour could also be said to reveal that she harboured some resentment at having to share attention with her unborn child. As we will see later in this book, this was a marriage where both sides started out thinking they would get the best out of each other but ended up getting the worst. Joyce's neediness was so ingrained – whether it was caused by a genetical flaw or from her past experiences – she could never change. She more-or-less ducked the question regarding her seizures during pregnancy when asked by Stone Phillips during a TV interview. When he wondered if there was a possibility that she had forgotten them, Joyce became a tad agitated, responding with:

'It's *not* possible I don't remember them. I remember everything about my first pregnancy. I don't remember what medications were described. I just took the medicine the physician or doctor [Dr Dean Spyres] prescribed for me. For the most part I was healthy. There was *nothing* out of the ordinary as far as my pregnancy was concerned.

'Jeff was raised with all the love and care that any child *could* be raised with and what happened to him I don't know. I wish I knew. I would give anything to know. I ask the universe why would this be allowed to happen. I don't have an answer for that.'

Perhaps Joyce had conveniently forgotten that on one occasion she is said to have attempted suicide with Equanil – a tranquiliser she had become addicted to.

Before we go further down this rocky marital road, for whatever reason one might wonder why the couple got married in the first instance. We don't know how long their engagement lasted but surely Joyce would have known that Lionel was a go-getter who analysed and thought carefully about every next move. He admits that he was self-centred, a workaholic, totally devoted to his career, his studies, perhaps unable to recognise frailty in others. It's likely that he had little time to pay attention to his son who later described his father – with a very rare touch of bitterness – as 'highly controlling with a strong character'.

On the other hand, Joyce was pathologically 'needy', appearing at face value to be emotionally attached but lacking any true empathy. Such people can be very selfish because they only cling to others or appear to need them to make themselves feel better. All of this is writ large throughout the narratives of both Lionel and his ever-demanding wife, so maybe she wanted a child for all the wrong reasons.

Joyce had always suffered frequent bouts of depression, nonetheless, she was successfully able to conceal much of this under a veil of over assertiveness, which manifested itself in an over-solicitous and totalitarian style. In order to survive emotionally, it comes across to us that Joyce was capable of 'splitting off' from her weaker self. She used denial and repression, which broadly speaking means, when one is not happy with a situation, one puts the conscious thought out of one's mind – very much in the same way as she did in the Stone Phillips interview. This was her mental defence mechanism, a vital requirement as, to her mind, Lionel further aggravated everything with his almost pathological focus on his career – *not* on her.

Perhaps Joyce thought that she would be better off if there was someone who really needed her, and, in turn, she could satisfy herself by having a child, 'an object' at her disposal; an object which could be controlled, manipulated and become totally reliant and centred on her. She perhaps wondered if the total love from Lionel she could not find in her married life could be found in a child?

Lionel's devout Christian grandmother, Catherine was very much of the 'old school'. From the rare accounts she has given she believed from the outset that Lionel and Joyce were ill-suited. 'Joyce was loud, argumentative and selfish,' she told one of the detectives who later interviewed her. 'They fought like cat and dog. It upset my home and my life. I'm sure that Lionel didn't want a child, not at first. He was starting a new career. He didn't have any money, but she was insistent. That's the only reason I allowed them to stay with me until he got on his feet.' Indeed, in one of her many attention-seeking attempts, one evening during the ice-cold, snowy New Year, the then pregnant Joyce stormed out of the house in nightgown without boots and walked a few blocks to a park. There she lay shivering in tall grass until Lionel came to collect her. Her doctor scolded her for being so petulant.

Having read much of the literature concerning Jeff Dahmer, I was surprised at the scarcity of information regarding Jeffrey's first years. It is as if those documenting the boy's early narrative have skipped over perhaps the most important time in a child's life. A baby's first experiences are all too important, and there was one experience of the very young Dahmer that would have shaped him – the leg casts. Jeffrey was born with clubfoot, a birth defect that makes one or both of a baby's feet point down and turn in. This is usually fixed with a leg cast. Without going into detail, the casting method involves the baby's foot being gently manipulated into a better position and then being put in a cast. A baby's tendons bend and stretch very easily. The leg is recast weekly for around five to eight weeks. After this stage, a tenotomy (small surgical incision) of the Achilles tendon is performed under local anaesthetic. Two-thirds of babies with clubfoot are male. Dahmer was also fitted with heel lifts to correct a leg length discrepancy – another orthopaedic problem that usually appears in young children. 'So what?' you might say. 'Millions of babies are born with clubfoot and have to have casts and wear heel lifts for several years, but they don't turn into serial killers, do they?' And one would be correct. But this is to miss the point I am about to make, for Jeffrey's birth deformities were only the first part of the 'layer cake' of both physical, psychological, familial, maybe even genetic problems.

Joyce wasn't unique in having struggled with mental illness during pregnancy. As many as one in five women have mental health problems in pregnancy or after birth, so Joyce was amongst many – it can happen to anyone. Depression and anxiety are the most common mental health problems in pregnancy. We also know that Joyce did not take well to breastfeeding. This activity 'made her nervous and irritable', writes Brian Masters, 'so she gave it up and bound her breasts.' It was Joyce's decision to wean her son cold turkey, but whether it was a deliberate action, or could not be helped, sudden weaning can have more of an effect on the mother, her body, mind, and on the baby, than one might realise. The sudden withdrawal of sustaining contact may have had an effect on baby Jeff. Some babies take this change in their stride, others do not. However, I think we find perhaps another problem here – not physical but psychological – to add to this infant's layer cake of problems.

Attachment is a deep emotional bond that a baby forms with the person who provides most of their care (usually the mother). A 'secure attachment', forms when a mother responds to her baby's needs consistently in warm, sensitive ways. Holding, rocking or talking softly to the baby all help promote attachment which helps provide a solid base from which a baby – in this case 'Baby Jeff' – can explore the world. It makes a baby feel safe and secure and helps them learn to trust other people. It's the basis of setting the good example that we explored earlier. A mother who is depressed – as Joyce was – may have trouble responding consistently to her baby in a loving and caring way. I stress, I am not implying that she did not *try* to give 'Baby Jeff' the best care, but for reasons that she didn't understand, she was unable to give that kind of care all the time. Mothers who suffer from depression can lead to an 'insecure attachment', which can cause problems for the child during infancy and later in childhood. Babies who do not develop this secure attachment may have trouble interacting with their mother – they may not want to be with their mother or may be upset when with them. It can cause children to be withdrawn, become passive, or develop slower than other babies. Simply put, babies need consistency from their mother's nurturing and if this is erratic or suddenly completely withdrawn, the child becomes unsettled. When he or she feels safe and loved one moment then abandoned and rejected the next it can cause a child to become unsettled. Toddlers and pre-schoolers can also be less independent and less likely to interact with other people including their peers. They might have more trouble accepting discipline, be more aggressive and destructive, or not do as well at school.

This kind of behaviour is writ large throughout Dahmer's narrative. At school, Jeffrey had behavioural problems, severe learning difficulties, a high attention deficit aligned with hyperactivity disorder and did not really excel at school or at anything after leaving school.

Even as a young child, he was in the high-risk category for anxiety, depression and other mental health problems. Research published in the journal *JAMA Psychiatry*, showed that depression may have a genetic link. A later study suggests a mother's mental health while pregnant can affect her child even more directly. Rebecca M. Pearson, PhD, and her colleagues at the University of Bristol in the UK, used data from more than 4,500 patients and their children in a community-based study. The researchers concluded that children born to depressed mothers were, on average, one-and-a-half times more likely to be depressed at aged eighteen. Pearson concluded: 'While shared genetic risk is one potential explanation, the physiological consequences of depression experienced by the mother can pass through the placenta and may influence the foetus's brain development. At an individual level the risks are very small. Having said this, these differences are meaningful at a population level.' Jeffrey Dahmer began to experience symptoms of severe depression at around the age of fifteen to sixteen.

Duncan Campbell in his book, *Murder in Mind: Jeffrey Dahmer the Milwaukee Serial Killer*, says that Jeffrey was: '...generally doted upon as an infant and toddler by both parents.' Adding almost as an afterthought, '...although the matriarch was known to be tense, greedy for attention and pity, and argumentative with her husband and their neighbours.' You are right on the money there, Duncan.

Like a lot of new parents, Joyce began a scrapbook in which she lovingly recorded every movement the baby made. In it she remarked that she and Lionel were 'scared' by his having correctional casts on his legs from birth until he was four months old, but that in the end 'all was fine'. '[He] would only need one and one eighth of an inch lifts on his shoes up to the age of six ... otherwise he was absolutely perfect,' she noted.

Jeff had his first accident very early, when he fell from his walker, skinning his hands and cutting his chin. In later divorce proceeding papers, Joyce would blame this on the lack of attention Lionel was giving to his son. Once again, we see denial and a transference of blame coming from Joyce.

According to both his parents, Jeffrey's first smile was recorded at a few weeks old. 'He stood up unaided at six-and-a-half months,' Joyce said. Aged eight-and-a-half months he was crawling and showing his first tooth. So far so good. He was even given two mild 'pats' on the bottom at nine months, then his first haircut. Of interest is that baby Jeff showed an interest in animals much earlier than expected or was usual. He was given a goldfish and a pet turtle when he was eighteen months old. 'Jeff was so gentle with the turtle,' wrote Joyce, 'as he explored like many a little boy, his relationship with another living creature.' On 25 November, 1961, it is recorded that Jeff walked unaided for the first time. 'I had to chase him to put him to bed,' Joyce penned proudly in her diary. But all was not as idyllic as it appeared.

The young family had by then rented a furnished apartment in Milwaukee where Lionel would begin reading for his master's degree in Analytical Chemistry at Marquette University. Living closer to campus made sense and this had been Lionel's decision and for his convenience, not Joyce's. As we have already noted, she was the type of woman who expected the world to revolve around her. According to Lionel, her response was to be expected. She claimed that the neighbours were a damned nuisance. Noise of any level to her was annoying and she bitterly complained in a disproportionate manner that she felt that her neighbours didn't belong in their own rooms. Lionel was constantly having to speak to the other tenants, asking them to keep their noise down to protect his wife's health – her mental health that is. This, quite rightly, was unwanted interference and the neighbours soon began shunning Joyce altogether. This was aggravation the hardworking Lionel did not need. To try and smooth things over with her husband, who was almost at his wits' end, Joyce kept the apartment spotless, ensuring that everything was in its place and pleasant. But the bottom line was this, she did so not for his delight, it was done so he would praise her for her domestic efforts. She needed perpetual reassurance that she was needed and adored.

In 1962 Lionel gained his Master of Science degree and was accepted at Iowa University to do postgraduate work towards a Doctor of Philosophy, which involved another upheaval for the family. They moved into a small house in Ames in Story County, Iowa. Ames is located some thirty miles north of Des Moines and is best known as the home of Iowa State University. Here, on 19 November 1966, Lionel would finally earn his doctorate in analytical chemistry.

When they moved in, the place was basically devoid of any furniture, but according to Joyce, 'Jeff didn't seem to mind. He was completely content in his bare room with his soft toys, doggie, muggsie, and his bed.' Apparently, there was a pet: 'Jiffy the Squirrel', who came to the windowsill looking for food and did not run away. According to Brian Masters, 'Mother and two-year-old son were photographed pointing at "Jiffy"; this kind of nature-fun did not happen in urban Milwaukee, and the child was fascinated. Soon he was watching all kinds of small animals and insects to see what they could do.' Lionel recalls:

> 'As a very young boy Jeff was very happy and he would run to me and jump up into my arms. He liked to ride his little tricycle and he liked very much to ride on the handlebars of my bicycle. When you look at the home movies you see a happy time. We had a very close relationship. He wanted to be held and he'd come running up to me whenever I came home from somewhere and he just loved to be with me and his mother, Joyce, who was very outgoing and liked to do new things, and she was a very loving person she seemed to me.'

It's notable that even in this recollection Lionel seems to doubt his judgement by qualifying his summary of his wife, as a mother, with the words 'she seemed to me'. Joyce recollected that time during an interview in 2017:

> 'Jeff was wonderful, wonderful. He was fun. We did all the normal things people do. If I had seen something that had been a clue to anything, I'd… I'd have done something, immediately. No. No, there was nothing wrong with Jeff.'

It's worth considering whether Joyce really never saw any warning signs that her son was different or whether she is taking shelter in denial. For what mother would want to admit that she saw the monster in her son at such a young age?

There have been many observers, both with a professional and passing interest in Dahmer's criminal narrative, who believe that Jeff's early interest in small creatures was the seed for his metamorphosis into a serial killer. This is simply an issue I don't buy into at all. A 2013 study was published by a team led by Vanessa LoBue from Rutgers University. The team investigated young children's interest in live animals. They carried out three studies where they put children in a naturalistic playing environment and gave them the choice to either play with animals or a set of very attractive toys. The results showed that children develop an interest in animals very early – usually between eleven to forty months old. The animals were in an enclosure for safety, so the children were not allowed to touch them but still preferred them to the static toys. Of course, it could have been the movement of the creatures that attracted the infants' attention, but we can conclude from the study results that the children interacted more frequently with the animals, even those like sleeping hamsters, than pretty toys. 'Toddlers prefer to look at an animal (even a snake or a spider) than play with a pile of attractive toys,' writes Mihai Andrei in an article summarising the study for *ZME Science*.[6]

As Professor Elliot Leyton might presume: 'Millions upon millions of toddlers across the world find small creatures fascinating but they all don't turn into serial killers, do they?' So we must not get our own minds in a tizz with the thoughts that even the most well-known forensic psychologists and psychiatrists consider, who suggest that young Dahmer's interest in living small creatures was, in some unique way, the cause of the terrible crimes he went on to commit in the years to come because that is a horse that could never run.

Joyce often claimed that she had felt hopeless and lonely as a child and that she felt a sense of abandonment by her father due to his alcohol abuse. Alcoholism has been linked to some specific genes. And, it is correct to say that having a close relative, such as a parent or sibling who struggles with alcohol disorder, increases the chances that a person will tussle with the same addiction. A 2008 study conducted by the National Institute on Alcohol Abuse and Alcoholism (NIAAA) concluded that hereditary genetic factors account for forty to sixty per cent of the variance amongst people who struggle with alcoholism. Jeffrey Dahmer would become an alcoholic by the age of fourteen. That is something to be considered but not the be-all and end-all, for Joyce was an attention-seeker who wallowed in self-pity, besides, we only have her word that her father was an alcoholic with nothing substantive to back that statement up!

It has been claimed by some writers that Jeff was deprived of attention as an infant. Willem H.J. Martens writing in his paper entitled *Sadism Linked to Loneliness: Psychodynamic Dimensions of the Sadistic Serial Killer Jeffrey Dahmer*[7] stated that in Dahmer's case there was:

'... a psychodynamic link between loneliness and sadism in the case of Jeffrey Dahmer: envy; shame/rage mechanism; a disturbed oral-sadistic development; castration fear; and severe feelings of inferiority; the conviction of being unlovable and unacceptable; need to diminish tension; powerful and oral-sadistic; inadequate and frustrated parenting, and reality distortion appear to be involved in sadistic aetiology.'

I was particularly taken with the 'oral-sadistic' part of Martens's summary of Jeffrey's psychopathology. Abraham Harold Maslow (1908-1970) was an American psychologist who was/is best known for creating 'Maslow's Hierarchy of Needs' – which needs a lot of study to get to grips with. And this is all about a theory of, '... psychological health predicated on fulfilling innate human needs in priority, culminating in self-actualization.' Now, I beg you to follow me for a tad longer because Maslow subdivided the oral stage into two parts:

1. an early oral phase dominated by the pleasure of sucking and described as 'preambivalent', because the breast is not yet conceived as at once good and bad, both frustrating and gratifying; and

2. an oral-sadistic or '*cannibalistic*' stage, occurring later, during the second six months of life, and contemporaneous with teething, which sees the emergence of the wish to bite and incorporate the object, destroying it in the process.

I did say that getting inside the head of Jeffrey Dahmer might become stressful, did I not? Nonetheless, Maslow adds:

> 'Instinctual ambivalence makes its appearance during the second phase, as incorporation becomes destructive. The oral-sadistic phase is thus characterized by the advent of aggressiveness, by ambivalence, and by the anxiety associated with the destruction of the loved object and the fear of being devoured in turn by that object. Elsewhere, in the context of a discussion of interaction, attention has been drawn to the way in which the child's cannibalistic instincts can revive those of the mother' (Golse, 1992).

Therefore, for whatever reason, what we do know is that Joyce suddenly denied her son breastfeeding and, while most babies will readily take to the comfort of the bottle, others may take the abrupt change in this, their tactile world, as rejection and Jeffrey has often said that he cannot cope well with disappointment.

There is one other huge event in infant Jeffrey's life that we must address. At the end of 1963, he was treated for an ear infection, mild pneumonia and diagnosed with a double hernia problem. An operation was required. About three to five per cent of healthy full-term babies are born with this condition. If not treated, it can cause serious problems. Jeff's symptoms were a full round belly, pain and soreness. Occasionally he vomited, he was fussy, there was a redness near the hernia, and he suffered bouts of fever – the poor mite.

Brian Masters records in his book about Dahmer that the boy was admitted to hospital in a state of apprehension. The operation would have been daunting enough for an adult and would have been quite terrifying for a little boy. The surgery was performed on Thursday, 19 March 1964, and when Jeff recovered from the anaesthetic, all he would have felt was intense pain in the groin where the incisions were made. Twenty-seven years later, Jeffrey told a Dr Judith Becker that the pain was so intense he thought his genitals must have been cut off. In her diary, Joyce noted that Jeffrey was 'so good in hospital … [but] he really disliked the doctor after this ordeal.' She says that she spent as much time as she could with him whilst he recovered in hospital. At night, he would say to her, 'You can go home now, Mommy, I'll sleep.' After the operation Jeffrey appeared markedly more vulnerable and subdued. During his slow and continued recovery at home he sat in complete silence in the living room for long periods, hardly stirring.

The pain lasted for about a week. Masters considers in his book whether Dahmer's young age meant that the operation took on a disproportionate significance in Dahmer's life going forward. The pain, the feeling of helplessness and perhaps violation would echo through Dahmer's life in later years. For a very long time, the operation would be the most significant event in his life. Of course, as Leyton would remind me, millions of very young children have hernia operations every year, but they don't all turn into serial killers, do they?

Brian Masters writes: '...by all accounts, Lionel was a quiet, reserved, undemonstrative young man, studious, austere with a quick temper when aroused,' and this comes across in the TV interviews he has given over the years. We may add that he's deeply introspective, too. Lionel himself has admitted that he himself is not perfect; that he was shy and bullied at school; that he often had strong thoughts about starting fires and hurting those who taunted him.

Whittier School, Ames

'When I was a little kid I was just like anybody else.'

Jeffrey Dahmer

Jeffrey Dahmer began his education aged five at the Whittier School, 124 S. Hazel Avenue, in Ames. He would catch the school bus to and from school with another lad called Kent. Joyce would later say that it sometimes broke her heart to send her son to school looking so 'forlorn and frightened.' We have little knowledge of his time at Whittier School, with the exception of a teacher's report suggesting, that she thought Jeff felt neglected. There was probably some truth in this. The teacher claimed that she detected early signs of abandonment, saying that Jeff was 'inordinately shy, always standing alone in the playground, profoundly unhappy … he arrived at school alone … maybe a few friends but so very few … he left the school alone. It was very sad to see the young boy looking so lost.' Lionel recalled, 'We visited the teacher, and we became very concerned, as she did, but I thought it was just shyness, as I had gone through when I was a youngster in school.' Adding wistfully, 'But this wasn't just shyness, it was total isolation which, in retrospect, proved true, *very* true.'

However, after lessons had ended, and at weekends, along with some of his peers he did what millions of lads do – go out to play and, on occasions, get into trouble. This was a poor area. Brian Masters notes in his book that it had 'a long tunnel under the bridge which they [the kids] liked to explore because it was dark and spooky.' Jeff had two pals – one white the other black – who lived across the railroad tracks, so Jeff had to walk through the tunnel to get to them. There were many derelict and deserted homes, and the residences were spread out with some distances between them. It seemed as if no one wanted to live here anymore so it was an ideal place to break a few windows and run like heck. Jeff soon came unstuck when the police turned up at the Dahmers' home saying that their son, now aged six, was one of a gang of tearabouts. Lionel and Joyce were ashamed and grounded their son as punishment. Jeff would spend much of his time playing in apple trees or on piles of coal and come home filthy, only to earn another scolding. His days were spent riding around on his cycle, playing hide and seek and 'ghosts in the graveyard' – just 'totally absorbed' recalls Lionel.

Another one of the lad's favourite places to visit was an animal research centre on the outskirts of Ames. He was fascinated, imagining that this was some kind of radiation testing facility and a magical world of living creatures. The men who worked there wore rubber gloves right up to their armpits. Jeff once saw a man with his arm right inside a cow's rear end. He discovered a long-deserted building, the steps of which were littered with dead mice and rats. Overcome with curiosity, he recalled: 'I walked up and wanted to see if the door was unlocked. I pushed the door open. I've never seen so many rats and mice running for the corners in my life. The whole floor was complete movement, it was just covered with them. I ran out of there pretty quick. They came out of the door, too.'

Around this time – Dahmer could not recall if he was aged four or five – he and another little boy found a hornets' nest in a crack in one of the facility's deserted buildings. Jeff told the kid to put his hand inside and see what he might find. 'There might be ladybugs,' he had suggested to his friend. The boy was seriously stung by the hornets, running home to tell his mother he'd been bitten by ladybugs. 'It was a rotten thing to do,' Dahmer later said.

Jeffrey's fascination and interest in animals continued into his childhood. He was surrounded by snakes, toads, crabs, fish and wild rabbits. The Dahmers also had a pet kitten called Buff. On one occasion, he was riding alongside his father on their cycles through the parking lot at the research centre when they spotted a baby nighthawk and took it home to raise it. 'It was almost like a pet,' Joyce later recalled. 'It would come back when you called it, eat out of your hand and stuff like that. We called him Dusty. The bird stayed until it was strong enough to fly and then,' said Joyce, 'it responded to our whistle even after it was gone three days.'

Although the year is uncertain – some say the Fall of 1964, others say 1965 – at some point, Lionel found the remains of animals, which had been killed by civets, in the crawlspace under their house. He placed them in a bucket and took them indoors where Jeff stared at them intently. According to Lionel, 'Jeffrey gathered the tiny bones and seemed oddly thrilled by the brittle, crackling sound they made as he repeatedly dropped them to the floor "like fiddlesticks". Jeffrey laughed and played with them endlessly. When he held some of his animals, he could feel their "fiddlesticks" inside, and wondered if they looked the same.'

Perhaps more ominously, at the same age Jeffrey pointed to his belly button and asked his father, 'What would happen if someone cut it out?' Lionel later wondered 'was that an ordinary question from a child starting to explore his own body or was it a sign of something dark already entering his mind?' And we might also ask, was there something macabre going on here in the mind of a child during his formative years? Maybe yes, maybe no. Lionel also recalls an incident when he took his young son fishing: 'Jeff was captivated by the gutted fish; staring intently at the brightly coloured entrails; was that a child's natural curiosity, or was it a harbinger of the horrors later to be found in apartment 213 [Jeffrey's later home]?'

There are claims that Dahmer tortured and even killed animals, but these are almost certainly untrue. Dahmer didn't kill a living creature – aside from the humans he would murder later on. Psychologists, Georgia Panagiotaki, Carys Seeley and Gavin Nobes, from the

University of East Anglia, wrote a paper on how young children approach and understand death.[8] 'Death is a fascinating subject to many children. For example, when they come across a dead creature or plant. Their observations and questions show a healthy curiosity as they strive to make sense of a complex world. Most pre-schoolers do not grasp the biological basis of death and tend to believe that death is a different state of life.' One of the big questions with Dahmer is whether his early interest in dead things was anything unusual and something to be concerned about.

As 1966 drew to a close, it appears that the years from three to six years old were the most enjoyable for young Dahmer. Thereafter, his parents' marriage became increasingly stormy. Jeff would become accustomed to the sight of his parents quarrelling, sometimes coming to the point of blows – and once when a knife was drawn – so his problems had only just started and far worse was yet to come.

Jeff was only six years old, and his mother was becoming more dysfunctional by the week. Joyce's hypersensitivity was also causing irritable allergies, skin rashes, hives, itches and fevers. She was also still struggling with depression. She felt lonely and hopeless. Her already low self-esteem plummeted, and she could find very few things to enjoy. She was tearful at the drop of a hat. And the arguments between her and the hapless Lionel were getting worse. Joyce turned to pills – lots and lots of different pills – to calm her down. Such was her state of mind that, as mentioned earlier, her memory of this time wasn't clear in later years. The medication didn't seem to work for Joyce. It is believed that she once again contemplated suicide. Lionel, who was struggling to finish his doctorate studies, also found himself responsible for most of the housework when Joyce was out of action. As Joyce didn't have a driving licence, he also did all of the shopping. On occasions Jeffrey saw his father hit his mother. It's no wonder young Jeff wanted to escape and venture out with his few pals into the woods to play – even if, when he came home dirty, he would get in trouble yet again.

Then a miracle happened... Joyce found Christ and the 'Church of Christ' which seemed as good a path to a quieter spirit as any. She and her husband were both baptised in that faith. It appears that any of a multitude of the Churches of Christ affirm the orthodox teachings of the person of Christ and the Bible as the sole rule of faith. Devotees practice with the primacy of the New Testament as the revelation of the Will of God, so this was at least an effort on her part to embark on a journey into the Light. Lionel said that things did calm down a bit after this. And he said that Joyce told him that she wanted another child. After the nightmare of her first pregnancy and the struggles she had been through in the previous years, his jaw must have dropped to the floor.

What must it have been like to have been in Lionel's shoes at this time? He was an aloof, quiet, studious guy – psychologically the polar opposite to his wife. Perhaps he thought that, with her newfound faith, she could now cope with the pressure of becoming pregnant again. If he did, this was blind optimism, for when Joyce became pregnant again their marriage started to go downhill faster than an Olympic skier. Lionel received his doctorate and started hunting around for a better job to support his growing family – one that would entail another move, another home and another school for young Jeffrey.

Hazel Elementary School, Barberton

PPG Industries' motto is: 'We protect and beautify the world'. PPG makes paint, you see. They were, and still are today, a global manufacturer of paints. And they feature in our psycho-travelogue because they gave Lionel Dahmer a job. Lionel's new job demanded that the family upped sticks again – this time to the village of Doylestown, Ohio, established in 1827 by one William Doyle.

If you are so inclined, it's worth reading about William Doyle – he comes across as someone of note, that is if you happen to live in Doylestown, a place I would die to visit – out of boredom. A blue-collar town, Doylestown sits on the outskirts of Akron – 'The Rubber Capital of the World'. It's the international headquarters of the giants of the rubber industry. They make a lot of rubber in Akron I can tell you this much. The first pneumatic tyres were made here, as was the first rubber-bound golf ball; the first tubeless tyre and the first US space suits. Doylestown is very big on rubber and not much else.

At first the Dahmers rented a place, and immediately the fractious Joyce started complaining about any noise the neighbours made. She eventually insisted that they move yet again. Brian Masters rightly points out that this was a rural area 'so the neighbours would have to be pretty loud to be heard at all.' Wringing her hands, she clutched Lionel's wrists and begged him to get her more pills when she ran out. She was now eating them like Smarties. To compensate for another move, they bought Jeff a dog. He named it Frisky. 'It was nice to have a companion like that,' he later recalled.

With Joyce unable to settle at the first place, they moved again to another rented house in Barberton. Joyce appeared to have no problem with the neighbours here. Jeffrey was enrolled at the Hazel Elementary School, and he did not like it. To start with he had to make new friends. One day, while messing around with a lad whom Jeff found particularly friendly, the boy asked Jeff to strangle him, only in jest, of course. Jeff squeezed. The kid broke free and ran straight back to his mother in tears. The child's mother reported Jeffrey to a teacher who gave him ten slaps with a paddle. Jeff Dahmer claimed that he was betrayed.

Another incident occurred at his Barberton school. There was a teacher he liked. 'I got kind of attached to her, so I thought I'd catch some tadpoles and give them to this teacher as a present. She said, "Thank You", and acted like she thought it was a great gift, so that made me happy. A day or so later, the tadpoles had gone missing from the classroom windowsill where she kept them. I just figured that she'd taken them home or something.' When Jeffrey visited a friend of his own age and who lived behind his own house, there in the garage, were the tadpoles in the very same container.' Jeffrey felt betrayed again, and then angry. Out of spite, he poured car engine oil into the container and killed all the tadpoles. If his teacher didn't want his gift, then no one else could have them.

Many observers claim that around this time young Dahmer was starting to exhibit signs of childhood schizophrenia. The condition is essentially the same as schizophrenia in adults, but starts, of course, early in life – generally in the teenage years. It's worth mentioning that schizophrenia in children younger than age thirteen is extremely rare. Schizophrenia can cause a range of problems with thought processes (cognitive), behaviour and emotions and patients interpret reality abnormally. They may suffer hallucinations, delusions. Their thinking becomes extremely disordered and impairs the child's ability to function. While the exact causes of schizophrenia are unknown, research suggests a combination of physical, genetic, psychological and environmental factors can make a person more likely to develop the condition. Schizophrenia often runs in families. Other causes are disturbed family relationships, childhood trauma and stress. With his own mother's struggles with mental health is it not beyond the realms of possibility that Jeff was also showing signs of mental disorders.

David Dahmer – Jeffrey was allowed to choose his baby brother's name – was born on 18 December 1966. With Lionel now settled into his great new job, the couple started planning for the future beginning with looking for a new, larger house. A Sunday drive was a treat for parents and kids alike, although principally this was for Joyce's benefit as otherwise she would simply be stuck at the house with little to do but think about her own problems. It was during one of these drives, in tranquil leafy Bath Township (population circa 10,000) that the ideal place caught their eye.

Today, 4480 W. Bath Road, Akron, appears like an ordinary, suburban ranch. A wooden porch runs along the eastern side of the stone-over-block residence and there is a separate two-car garage reached via a gravel driveway. The 250 feet by 300 feet lot slopes down east to west and, back then, water was gathered from the run-off by a spring which serviced the home. There is a living room, dining room, family room, kitchen, utility room, two bathrooms and three bedrooms. A small room adjacent to the living room contained a hot water tank and an oil-fired boiler. When the Dahmers bought it, it needed some maintenance inside and out. The couple raised a loan from the bank and bought the place. It was valued at about $58,000. Like other homes in this much-desired area, its value would appreciate substantially over the next twelve years – surrounding properties, even some vacant lots, are now selling for six figures. As far as my research tells me, 4480 W. Bath Road last sold in 2005 for $244,500 to Chris Butler, a man tied to the eighties pop culture as a songwriter and guitarist for the new wave band The Waitress, who were best known for the ironically titled hit song *I Know What Boys Like*.

Jeffrey had turned eight just four days after they moved in, but family life was turning even more sour. Joyce had been ill for some six months. Jeffrey would later say that, with his all-but-absent-father and his mother unable to care for herself properly let alone two boys, he 'felt neglected.' So already we are finding several negative conditions starting to affect the young lad – frequent changes of homes, a distant and authoritarian father, a temperamental and depressed mother – all perhaps becoming the basic ingredients of the psychological layer cake for all that would follow. And yet I can still hear Professor Leyton saying: 'So what? So what if his father wasn't around much and his mother was a pain-in-the-ass? Millions of children around the world experience a similar upbringing but they don't turn into cannibals, do they?'

Deep woodland can be a magical place for a young lad, and the house in sleepy Bath Township was right in the middle of what could be described as a small forest – you might enjoy looking at the aerial view online. There are some other houses nearby but there are thousands of trees. In summer, the trees in full-leaf create a canopy so that many of the area's roads are little more than shady tunnels. In such tranquil places, imaginations can grow and a boy who is shy and introverted can lose himself for hours amongst the trees and bushes – watching animals, tracking, learning. Jeffrey couldn't have hoped for a better place to escape the constant tensions and arguments at home. So, can we imagine eight-year-old Jeffrey now? It's quite nice to envisage this somewhat gangly lad – having moved home three times in two years, leaving his playmates behind, with a two-year-old brother – wandering around with his dog Frisky. Out in nature where no one could tell him what to do.

And, there were other things going on in Dahmer's life, too. By the age of ten, his fascination with the remains of animals had escalated and he had started to experiment with things that were once alive. He would stuff insects into bottles of formaldehyde and decapitate small mice or even rats. There were easy pickings for him in the road kills along West Bath Road, and in amongst the trees and undergrowth of deep woodland close by. He became adept at stripping the meat and fur from dead creatures. So here might arguably be the roots of what some may say is more than morbid curiosity.

For a while, Joyce Dahmer was in good spirits at their new home; bustling around, cleaning and polishing and proud that they'd moved to a more upscale property. Lionel built a chicken coop so they could have their own fresh supply of eggs, and Jeff even helped him raise sheep, rabbits and ducks on the land around the property. It was an ideal place to raise a family, but it might be fair to suggest that, by now any chance of repairing much of the earlier psychological damage had gone. Jeff had become a loner. Yes, later he paid a few visits to their neighbours, the Lehrs, nearby to take sled rides with their son Steven who was a year younger. But he had few friends and was quite withdrawn. Jeff took over Steven's paper round when he and his family went on holiday, but he lacked the confidence for taking on any meaningful responsibilities.

Watching his son develop, Lionel realised that something was amiss. Jeff rarely seemed interested in anything, save being left to his own devices in a world he was creating for himself. Children who are withdrawn rarely seek adult attention and avoid lively interaction with their peers. They may tag along on the edge of a group, but they prefer solitary play and like to disappear into a self-contained bubble. They can seem subdued, and it can be hard to get them to light up. All of this could be witnessed in young Jeffrey.

'This lack of social interaction in childhood may result from a variety of causes, including social fear and anxiety or a preference for solitude. From early childhood through to adolescence, socially withdrawn children are concurrently and predictively at risk from a wide range of negative adjustment outcomes,' as Kenneth H. Rubin, Robert J. Coplan, and Julie C. Bowker, write as abstract in 'Social Withdrawal in Childhood' *Annual Review of Psychology*. These negative outcomes include socio-emotional difficulties (e.g. anxiety, low self-esteem, depressive symptoms, and internalising problems), peer difficulties (e.g. rejection, victimisation, poor friendship quality), and school difficulties (e.g. poor teacher-child relationships, academic difficulties, school avoidance). Although social withdrawal is not a clinically defined behavioural, social, or emotional disorder in childhood it is not the display of solitude *per se* that may pose a problem; rather, the central issue is that social withdrawal may reflect underlying difficulties or a social or emotional nature. Indeed, Lionel, himself, admitted that he had probably left it too late to try and snap young Jeff out of this apparent lethargy, saying: 'I ought to have spent time with him long before.' Therefore, can we see how Jeffrey's emotional layer cake is deteriorating month by month? I certainly think one can.

Eastview Junior High School

'We are such stuff as dreams are made on, and our little life is rounded with a sleep.'

William Shakespeare, *The Tempest*

Jeffrey's next school was Eastview Junior High School. On the short yellow bus rides from and back to his home on West Bath Road Jeffrey made a few friends, but any friendships he did make were on a superficial level. One lad, who shared that ride with Jeffrey every morning, remembered him as being funny and kind of odd at the same time. He played the cornet in the school band for a while. According to Masters, Jeffrey 'habitually sat at the lunch table with Bill Henry, Greg Rogerson and David Borsvold, but was regarded by others as slightly odd. A smart kid, but really bizarre, or simply nice, quiet, reserved.'[9]

While his classmates had some difficulty in connecting with him, adults tended to like Jeff Dahmer. He was polite, neat and willing to please – flashing a gentle, shy smile when he was complimented. Georgia Scharenberg, who lived next door to the Dahmers, recalled Jeff as being 'a nice boy who spent his out-of-school hours prowling in the woods, climbing the stony ledges and dashing among the trees ... there were few playmates. Jeff was more or less with his brother all the time, and not with the other boys.' Other adults who knew Jeffrey agreed; that, if anything was marked about his behaviour in childhood, it was his politeness and good manners. However, he had a hard time keeping friends and, by the time he arrived at junior high, the overpowering loneliness that was to haunt his existence was already proving to be a red flag. The skinny, tow-headed kid with the big glasses was more than a bit geeky, he was clearly *very* different. Mrs Scharenberg worked as a cashier in the school's lunchroom, and recalled that when Jeff came through the queue, they would usually exchange a few remarks at the cash register before he carried his tray away. 'He would sit down with the other students at a table to eat,' she recalls, 'but when he left the room, he always left alone.' Indeed, Dahmer later confirmed that he was something of a loner, saying: 'I was never one to go out and voluntarily play football and baseball or anything like that. Group sports just didn't interest me.'

It is here that I observe something probably missed by many – an issue that will surely resonate later when we come to his many murders. I sense from all that we have thus far noted in Jeffrey's narrative, that it is not that he did not *want* friends in his peer group, it's that he was psychologically ill-equipped to make and *keep* close any real friends. Jeff was, without any doubt, withdrawn. Simply put, he craved friendship but ultimately, this shy, introverted young lad, just could not get it together and develop the social skills humans need. It didn't help that his family had moved around so much as any pals he had made in his previous schools were now left behind. The feelings of abandonment – almost of betrayal – had set in once again.

Perhaps Jeffrey's closest friend at this time was David Borsvold with whom he shared a common interest. Both lads were fascinated with geology and pre-history, seeking out and collecting rocks and pictures of dinosaurs. Masters notes most eloquently: 'Not even Jeff realised, then, that the drawings of dinosaur skeletons and bones answered to something deep in his psyche which the other boys could not share and would never suspect.'[10] Masters could be accused of making this observation with hindsight though. The fact is that tens-of-thousands of inquisitive kids are fascinated by dinosaurs and the idea of discovering ancient creatures through examining their remains. They might stand agog when first setting eyes upon the world-famous, roaring Tyrannosaurus Rex skeleton at the National History Museum in London. They might peer at the skull of a Triceratops before eating their lunchbox snacks, dropping their crisps among the fossils in the Dinosaurs Gallery. And, they don't all become psychopathic serial killers.

The friendship between Dahmer and Borsvold was a partnership of opposites. Borsvold was outgoing and gregarious to a fault. The lads became pals at school and were soon riding to and from each other's homes on their cycles. They competed in preparing displays for the science fair: David focusing on dinosaurs and Jeffrey on the various kinds of moulds and fungus to be found on and around his parents' property. Their work was proudly shown in a display case in the school's hallway. As the bond between the two lads steadily grew, Jeffrey started to feel safer, more confident and more trusting in David, certainly well enough to invite him into his own very private world.

In his solitary moments, which as we know were all too frequent, Jeffrey had dreamed up a game involving stick men and spirals. Brian Masters gives significant attention to this in his book although American author Don Davis pretty much skips over it in his history of Dahmer. In Jeff's game, the stick men constituted armies with each boy commanding one side. The stick men would be destroyed if they came too close to one another, writes Masters. Once annihilated, the stick men would disappear into spirals of nothingness. Nine-year-old Jeff called this 'Infinity Land'. Masters betters any psychologist or psychiatrist who had ever spent any time with Dahmer with his thoughts on this bizarre childhood activity:

> 'Jeff must not be credited with any major concept, but it is alarming that he should have used such a name for this childish exercise, and with hindsight it is possible to discern signs of which he was entirely unaware. The stick men were fleshless; they were not conceived with the full contours of people, but with the bare essence of bone. Their danger lay in closeness; any contact resulted in oblivion, suggesting that intimacy was the ultimate disaster, and the severest risk. The oblivion was represented by the black hole of infinity, an abject, featureless,

hopeless nothingness, which, perhaps the infant already saw when he gazed into himself. Or perhaps he saw it as the danger facing anyone who got near him.'[11]

I think that Brian Masters's perceptive observation is one of the most insightful into Dahmer's mind at this time as any. It is sheer brilliance. No fancy 'shrink talk', just distilled thinking. Yet, Masters draws back, by saying: 'All of which is, of necessity, fanciful, for we cannot know whence the boy dredged this curious game; we can only conjecture, and must do so,' but does he *have* to conjecture, maybe not?

Of course, Jeffrey's Infinity Land was fanciful and possibly the result of an overactive imagination. The stick men were fleshless and without the full contours of people but, in psychology, imagination generally refers to the ability to *mentally* represent sensations that are not physically present. Indeed, anomalies of imagination are frequent and can be handicapping in most cases of schizophrenia spectrum disorders (SSDs). Dare we suggest that this boy was harbouring a subconscious curiosity, a desire to know, to see, or to experience something morbid? I think that we can because we know that, by this time, Jeffrey had already retreated into his own, private world – playing alone in the woods, frightened to go home to face his parents who were at each other's throats. He had a father who had little time for him and a mother who was mentally unbalanced for much of the time. It's almost too awful to contemplate that here we find Jeff now mentally seeding with his 'Infinity Land', something that would become reality before long:

real people with living flesh and bone contours who would meet their destruction when they came into close contact with him.

But soon the proverbial shit was about to hit the proverbial fan. One evening, two years after starting junior high school, the Dahmer family had chicken for dinner. Afterwards, Jeff asked his father what might happen if the leftover chicken bones were placed in bleach. Lionel recalled that he was intrigued that his now ten-year-old son should ask such a question. I know that if he had been my boy who had asked the very same question after a Sunday roast I would have told him to go help his mother to wash the dishes. Wouldn't you? But no, not Lionel. He put this curious question down to 'commendable scientific curiosity', and he was happy that Jeff was showing 'initiative'. Well, ya'll all know, I was brought up in the old school. One sat down at the table and ate all put in front of you. If you ask my sister, Lizzie, she will tell you that we didn't leave the table until you cleaned the plate. Imagine the dinner conversation:

> Me: 'Dad, I can't eat anymore. I'm full up.'
> Dad: 'Your mother has spent a long time cooking this meal. The Brussel sprouts are good for you. Look, Christopher, your sister has eaten all of hers and has left the table. Now finish yours.'
> Me (unblinking): 'Dad, what happens if I put all them chicken bones in some bleach?'
> Dad: 'Now, my lad, that's an interesting question, one that raises some scientific curiosity to

my mind. But here's the thing, son. Your mom is washing the dishes so eat those Brussel sprouts, then haul ass and start drying the plates.'

Of course I made all of that up, honest to God I did. I did warn you, from the outset, that my subconscious mind does, on its own accord, and without any reference or invitation to my conscious thinking, sometimes wander off into a fanciful tangent just to lighten the load. Maybe it's because the only Christmas cards I get are from various Death Row inmates.

Revere High School

Our psycho-travelogue has brought us to the final part of young Dahmer's education at Revere High School. By now, he had discovered alcohol, which soothed his troubled mind. By the age of fourteen, he was already staggering along the road into alcoholism. He would drink anything he could get his hands on, including neat Scotch.

Without wishing to state the obvious, the effects of alcohol on young people are not the same as they are for adults. While alcohol misuse can present health risks and cause careless behaviour in *all* age groups, it is even more dangerous for young people. A particularly useful paper to read on this subject is *Alcohol's Effects on the Adolescent Brain*[12] from the National Institute on Alcohol Abuse and Alcoholism and can be found online. The paper states that specifically for children and young people under age eighteen, alcohol acts as a depressant that affects the brain by causing the cognitive system to slow down. Without intervention and abstinence it will affect the developing brain into the early twenties, thus negatively impacting on problem solving skills and performance at school. According to the National Health and Medical Research Council (NHMRC): 'The earlier a person starts drinking alcohol at harmful levels the greater the risk of changing development of the brain. This can lead to problems with memory and learning and increases the risk of having alcohol-related problems later in life.' There is much evidence of the damage drinking did in Dahmer's schooling history – as well as into his later years while he was committing multiple sado-sexual homicides.

There are two parts of the brain significantly affected by alcohol during the teenage years because of the momentous changes youngsters are undergoing at this time:

- The hippocampus is responsible for memory and learning. Studies of adolescents show that heavy and extended alcohol use is associated with a ten per cent reduction in the size of the hippocampus. The studies also show that the function of the hippocampus is uniquely sensitive to alcohol at and during the teenage years and that alcohol may be poisonous to the nerve cells of the hippocampus causing them to be damaged or destroyed.
- The prefrontal lobe is important for planning, judgement, decision making, impulse control and language. It is the area of the brain that changes the most during the teenage years. Research has shown that heavy drinking adolescents have smaller prefrontal lobs than young people of the same age who do not drink.

Alcohol is a toxin; its primary impact on the body – especially when consumed excessively – is obviously harmful. Heavy drinking or binge drinking for five or more days in a month, can lead to long-term brain damage that simultaneously damages other parts of the body. Research shows that sustained periods of drinking lead to overall shrinkage of the brain. Remember that Dahmer started drinking around the age of eleven or twelve and he was binge drinking by the age of fourteen.

When alcohol enters the body, it travels from the stomach to the intestines and through the bloodstream to various organs. In the liver, spikes in blood alcohol content caused by heavy drinking overload its ability to process alcohol. So, excess alcohol journeys from the liver to other parts of the body, like the heart and central nervous system. Subsequently, alcohol moves through the blood-brain barrier, affecting the brain's neurons directly. There are approximately eighty-six billion interconnected neurons in the brain and central nervous system.

Jeffrey Dahmer later admitted that he turned to alcohol to escape the pain of his parents' constant arguing, bickering and then the trauma of their acrimonious divorce. The only way he could blot this upheaval out was to enter a world of his own. He needed to escape reality, so he turned to the mood-altering substance, alcohol, as a way to find relief from his problems. However, the more he turned to drink for relief, the more troubled he became. His school had noticed and informed Lionel Dahmer. His father had a few words with him but made no real attempt to help Jeffrey. As Lionel, himself, has said: 'Jeff would come home drunk from high school. The drinking got worse and worse, and I talked about it with him – of the dangers of continuing but at that point he was so addicted physically and mentally.' Dahmer's brain was chemically primed for escapism. Although this will seem obvious, escapism is generally defined as behaviour to ignore, evade, or avoid reality. Jeff Dahmer needed a mental diversion from the unpleasant and boring aspects of his daily mundane life. He desperately needed to occupy himself away from the persistent feelings of depression and general sadness.

We know that Jeff showed an interest in the remains of dead animals from the age of four. And we know that by the time he became a ten-year-old he had started building, what he called his 'bug collection': butterflies; moths; dragonflies; mantises, spiders and beetles that he preserved in formaldehyde. Although at first Lionel – a highly-talented chemist – denied he'd taught his son how to preserve animals he later confessed that he had. Jeffrey had soon moved on to larger creatures. He would peer closely at these dead creatures, through his spectacles; picking up a small, sharp knife and tweezers, he would gently pry their bodies apart. Intent in his own bubble world, this lonely lad would have been totally focused as he delved deeper into what had once been a small living, breathing entity, to see how all the bits and pieces fitted together as a whole. Maybe he felt like a pseudo-pathologist as he stripped birds and rats of their flesh. Perhaps, reducing animals to skeletons provided an outlet for his growing aggression and perhaps satisfied a need for self-assertion. Occasionally accompanied by one or more of his few pals, he dismembered the carcasses either at home or in nearby woodland and stored the parts in jars in the family's tool shed. He later explained that he grew 'very curious as to how animals fitted together.'

On one occasion he brought home a piglet's head and stripped off the flesh to examine the skull. He later said that he received no sexual pleasure from these dissections but admitted that they gave him a 'sense of control'. So, can you see Jeffrey now? I can. He was developing a paraphilia, that is a sexual arousal from these activities – a grim fascination with the dead. Maybe here we see a teenager who has little to no control over the living, so exerts it over the dead – another ominous portent for the terrible events to come.

Lionel has gone on record with his recollections of his own early days. He spoke of his fears, and his dreams of killing the people who bullied him at school.[13] Lionel considered the idea that he may have passed on destructive genes to Jeffrey. After his son's arrest he spoke about his struggle to come to terms with what his son had done: 'It has been internal torment. As I began to confront Jeff's childhood days imagining it became clear to me that they had not always been wholly different [imaginings] from my own. The same needs, impulses, lived a shadowy half-life in me.' These are statements that we cannot lightly dismiss. We must consider the psychopathology of Lionel Dahmer himself when we come to decide if this in any way, impacted upon Jeff Dahmer as a very young boy.

At this time, Joyce's already fragile state of mental health totally collapsed. Back came the uncontrollable shakes, an ever-increasing reliance on drugs, often as many as eight Equanil a day along with laxatives and the dependency on sleeping pills. This caused an already strained marriage to deteriorate even more. 'It just didn't seem like my parents really didn't like each other too much,' recalled Jeffrey.

'It made me feel on edge, unsure of the solidarity of the family. I decided early on I wasn't going to get married cos I never wanted to go through anything like that.'

Of course there were fun days in the sunshine when the family went on long walks together, putting notches on a staff to indicate how many miles they had walked. They would visit garden centres to buy plants for their garden. Yet Jeffrey saw this as being a pretence to appear as if all was normal in his parents' marriage – for him, it was a sham and a scam. Besides he preferred to be left to his own devices and not be in the company of his mother and father, who were always bickering and arguing. 'When she was on the medication – which seemed like years to me – most of the time she'd be too tired to do anything … she just seemed to be in bed most of the time we were in Bath Township,' Jeffrey confirmed. 'The atmosphere in the house was bad, a good deal of shouting and hurling of objects occurred.' (Although he and his younger brother were never assaulted.)

So what psychological impact did all of this have on Jeffrey Dahmer? Part of the answer lies with Lionel Dahmer: a quiet, studious man with a scientific mind, although somewhat aloof it is fair to say. He was the breadwinner after all is said and done but he was also a father who admits he had little time for Jeffrey. Lionel was career-minded and focused on only the tangible. For her part, Joyce Dahmer was intangible. Her moods were unpredictable, she was needy and complained constantly – about anything, even trivial issues. Her constant demands for attention from her husband, who was already at his wits' end, meant that she had little time for her two sons.

So, we can see why Jeffrey Dahmer sought his own company, to find a quiet place where his fantasies could flourish and grow. He could not talk to his father, who had no time for him, and he could not talk to his mother, who didn't have the capacity to adequately care for herself let alone her sons. Joyce had even been sectioned in 1970 and spent a month in a mental hospital, followed by a course of psychotherapy over a period of another month. Yet this, and the continued taking of medication didn't help. Lionel Dahmer later ruminated on how his wife's mental health issues must have affected Jeffrey:

> 'Our marriage was starting to dissolve, and I told Jeff that Joyce was advocating for a divorce. We fought often and knives were drawn. Jeff reacted badly. He went out and started slapping trees with a branch, apparently because he felt like he was losing control. And he was obviously frustrated by it. Looking back on those times it makes me sick. Really sick. It makes me feel that we didn't really have a good family and I will feel this way till my death.'

Jeffrey's recollections of the demise of his parents' marriage paint the same picture:

> 'I started shutting down during the divorce proceedings. It was my way of shutting out painful thoughts; just taking an attitude of not caring about the pain that was going on with the divorce. This was effective. It worked. Maybe

my problems started then. There was incessant fighting between my parents. It was unnerving, depressing. It made me angry sometimes. I'd leave the house. Go out in the woods, sulk, brooding, wondering why they had to have such a rough relationship.'

Let's give pause for thought a moment. I'm not going soft at all but here we have a very young kid with a domineering father who was absent *much* of the time, and a mother who was neurotic *all* of the time. We are reminded of the cocktail of drugs prescribed Joyce during her pregnancy with Jeffrey. Could this toxic ingestion, as Lionel feared, have affected the foetus in any way? It's something not to be dismissed lightly.

Earlier in this book we established that, amongst the FBI's negative influences or predictors that can affect a child and create serial killers, is a dysfunctional home life. Yes, Jeff was not born on the wrong side of the tracks, but it's worth remembering that we never really know *what* goes on behind closed doors and curtained windows – even more so when a home is set deep in woodland away from prying eyes. If we were to put ourselves into that lad's shoes at this time in his life – and I say that we *should* if we are to try to understand him – how would one feel? Mum and Dad constantly fighting and almost coming to blows – even threatening each other with kitchen knives? Can you see a little further into the lad's mind now? Can you start to understand why he sought some solace, a bit of peace and quiet in the surrounding woods in his desperate effort to escape the mayhem indoors? I can.

And I also see him escaping into a bubble world all of his own – a place where fantasies, often dark fantasies, can be born and nurtured.

Brian Masters makes yet another very astute observation in his book *The Shrine of Jeffrey Dahmer*, when he says that Jeff's response to all of this was to blame himself for his mother's illness. He was projecting all of his later psychological problems onto himself in a self-mirroring sort of way. Jeffrey must have surmised that, because for as long as he could remember his mother had been depressed it must have been his birth that caused the illness. And it must be him who was the cause of this new relapse.

Dahmer went on to speak of this guilt and self-blame for his mother's troubles after his arrest. But this sense of guilt alone cannot explain the psyche of the man who committed such terrible murders. And even if Dahmer carried some of the genetic weight of his mother's mental predisposition – that also cannot be the single cause. There cannot be a *single* issue at work when it comes to a mind like Dahmer's – there must be numerous issues the maths of which culminate, layer-upon-layer, in forming a sexual serial murderer. So, Jeffrey Dahmer blaming himself for his mother's psychological problems post-arrest is nothing but hand-wringing. For Dahmer, this self-blame must have come from a false belief in control. Self-blame and the idea that they are somehow responsible for things they are not, can lead individuals – especially mentally fragile youngsters – to try their hand at unsolvable problems. In Dahmer's case, this was his parent's oncoming divorce – something that was all brought about by his mother's fragmented state of mind. I suggest, therefore, that while all alone in his own bubble world, there was never a self-blaming thought going through his mind. This came much later while he was trying to excuse himself for what he did – simply putting icing sugar onto a layer cake that was already stale from the outset. Of interest to us is, that he does not mirror his father's own shortcomings, that the evidence proves beyond any doubt that genetics had some part to play in all of this; that he was the product of parents who were predisposed to a failed marriage almost from the get-go.

At school, fuelled by the alcohol he now came to rely on, Dahmer was the class clown and used to entertain his peers with pranks. These activities became known as 'Doing a Dahmer'. Jeffrey would make bleating noises, simulate seizures or the symptoms of cerebral palsy and deliberately knock over items at school and in local stores. His sense of humour was grotesque, sometimes cruel. However, Dr Mike Kukral, Dahmer's long-time friend at Revere High School, has fond memories of Jeffrey:

> 'I don't think any of us thought of Jeff Dahmer as a bad guy in high school or a different person. The "Jeff Dahmer Fan Club" was a small group of us who thought that he was a funny kid. He was into pranks and doing goofy things. My favourite thing that Jeff did was in the library, and we had a pretty tough librarian. Jeff would be sitting with his face in a book not even looking up, and he would shout at the top of his lungs, real fast and really loud, and the librarian would jump up and say: "Who *did that*? Who is *that*?"

Never, never ever did she even suspect it was Jeff Dahmer. He could get away with things for a long time and never get caught. And we all learned that later from him too.'

There was, however, one weird incident that did puzzle Mike:

'One day I'm standing there in the hallway and Jeff rushed up and put his head on my chest, and I'm like: "Hey, what are you doing? What's going on?" And he stands up straight and says: "I wanted to know what your heart sounds like," and then he ran way down the hall.'

Another of Dahmer's favourite pranks was to sneak into group school photos. Again, Mike Kukral recalls:

'They took photos of all the groups at Revere High – sports and clubs whatever else – and Jeff sneaked into the photos when he was not a member of those groups. The funniest one is the National Honours Society, which is the brightest kids, the smartest kids – and definitely in our senior year Jeff Dahmer was *not* in the group academically. But he's in that group photo, and I believe that the president of that group had Jeff blacked out with a marker. So, in all of the yearbooks there is this body without a head, and it was one of the first things I thought about when he was arrested. I just remembered this strange photograph that is so haunting today to look at and knowing this person right there standing in the middle is Jeffrey Dahmer.'

Milwaukee psychiatrist Ashok Bedi, then director of the Milwaukee Psychiatric Hospital, has since speculated that this 'blotting out' had a 'traumatic effect on Jeffrey,' leading him later to experience the urge to 'blot out' the lives of others – 'to remove them from society.' But, to me, this hypothesis doesn't seem to hold any water at all. Far from trying to blot his victims out of his life, Dahmer wanted to keep, cherish and eat parts of them so they would always be a part of him. Ashok Bedi is totally correct, however, in saying: 'There was no obvious touchstone in Dahmer's past that can be pointed to as the event that created a serial killer.' Bedi partly hits the nail on the head but misses and strikes his thumb with this observation. With most multiple murderers, there is never one 'obvious touchstone' that creates a serial killer but rather an accumulation of events that work to complete the homicidal equation. Most of the serial killers I have interviewed in person and corresponded with at length, have gone through a sort escalation of behaviour, often starting in a sort of sex crime apprenticeship and visited many asocial waypoints before they graduated into fully-fledged monsters.

One example of a classic escalation can be found in my book, *Talking with Serial Killers*: Michael Bruce Ross. As a teenager, with an IQ of 150, Ross already had an insatiable sex drive. He was heavily into reading porn, demanded sex of his first girlfriend at least five times a day and yet still he masturbated to satisfy his needs. His next stage was to start stalking pretty girls around the Cornel University campus. Unable to control himself, Ross eventually carried out several sexual assaults then committed his first rape, then another rape and another rape with cooling off periods in between the attacks. Every time he would promise himself never to do anything like it again. Ultimately – completely in the grip of committing episodic violence – he raped and killed student Dzong Ngoc Tu and went on to kill a further seven young women aged fourteen to twenty-five. His counsellor Anne M. Cournoyer told me during a TV interview that, even whilst on Death Row at Somers Prison, Connecticut, 'he masturbated to the thoughts of his kills up to forty times a day which brought about bleeding sores on his penis.' Of Anne, Michael said: 'If I was in the right place in here and she in the wrong place in here, I could rape and kill her, and I'd love to.' Michael was priapic – there is no doubt about that. Jeffrey Dahmer, like other serial killers, followed a path of escalation that was a little different, but a path, nonetheless.

Jeffrey has a high IQ, but his school grades were usually low – a sure sign of early emotional disturbance and inability to concentrate. The pending divorce of his parents certainly left him with a feeling of having nowhere to turn to satisfy his emotional needs or express unhappiness. There was also a sense that he was autistic and incapable of feeling any real connection with his peers and other people.

Dahmer was never diagnosed with any form of autism, but some experts have identified certain traits that might suggest that he had Asperger's Syndrome including:

bizarre or erratic behaviour; a flat facial expression and flat monotonous speech; a mechanical gait (it was said that Jeffrey walked as though his knees were locked); and, of course, difficulty forming relationships and trouble interacting socially. It's worth stressing that not every individual diagnosed with either autism or Asperger's goes on to commit murder though.

From his Revere High School freshman year onwards, Jeffrey Dahmer was seen by most of his peers as an outcast with few friends. Many later recollected being disturbed by his drinking. He drank both beer and spirits, which he smuggled into school inside the lining of his army fatigue jacket then concealed in his locker. Alcohol consumption occurred before, during, and after classes. On one occasion a classmate watched as the bespectacled Jeff drank a cup of gin and asked him why he was drinking liquor in class. Dahmer casually replied, 'It's my medicine.' Nonetheless, during this period, although largely uncommunicative, Dahmer was observed by staff to be a polite student known to be highly intelligent, yet still he achieved only average grades which staff attributed to his apathy.

In his later police interviews, Jeffrey Dahmer says that he masturbated at least three times a day – something that mirrors the habits of Michael Ross, Ted Bundy and other emerging serial killers such as Kenneth Bianchi aka 'The Hillside Strangler' whom I interviewed at the Washington State Penitentiary, (WSP) Walla Walla, WA. When Jeff reached puberty he discovered that he was homosexual but did not divulge his sexual orientation to his parents. He did engage in a brief relationship with another youth:

'We did not have intercourse,' Jeffrey said. When asked by Stone Phillips if he had *ever* discussed his emerging homosexuality with his father, Jeff Dahmer gave this rather sad account of why he did not: 'My father and I never really had a heart-to-heart talk about what was going on inside our own minds. It was a hush-hush taboo subject. One *not* to be talked about, or even to be *thought* about. I just kept it all within me.' Later, Lionel was adamant about how he *would* have reacted had his son confided in him:

> 'I would have started him [Jeff] on a programme
> to try to change his thinking, I would *not* have
> accepted him. If you believe in the inspired word
> of God, homosexuality is a sin, which I do. Jeff
> lives in sin … it's repugnant.'

But Lionel, the Bible-thumper, slipped up here because the biblical authors had no notion of sexual orientation – the term 'homosexual' wasn't even coined until the nineteenth century. For people of faith, the Bible is looked to for timeless guidance on what it means to honour God with our lives; and this most certainly includes our sexuality. But preacher Lionel's assumption is all wrong! Indeed, poor Jeffrey, who was surely aware of his father's views, could have found solace in Psalm 27:10: 'For my father and my mother have forsaken me but the Lord will take me in.' One would be hard-pushed to find any church that is not compassionate about homosexuality. Even the Dahmers' own church is full of understanding for same sex relationships, something that Lionel conveniently forgets.

Young Dahmer was now reading porn and bondage magazines. He later admitted to police that it was at this time that he began to have sexual fantasies that included dominance and control over a completely subservient partner. This thinking process, this slow psychosexual metamorphosing, became entwined with his fascination with dissection. Another waypoint was looming on the horizon. In 1976, when Jeff Dahmer was around sixteen years old, he conceived a rape fantasy of rendering a male jogger he regularly saw, whom he found attractive, unconscious and making use of his unconscious body. One day he concealed himself in bushes on the route the normally jogger took. Baseball bat in hand, he lay in wait. However, on this particular day the jogger did not pass him by. Jeffrey later told police that this had been his first attempt to carry out an attack on a young man and that he had wanted to knock him out and lay with him. Dahmer had now entered a stalking phase. Stalking often becomes evident in some form or another in almost all criminal narratives of serial sexual offenders. My book *Talking with Serial Killers: Stalkers*, discusses in depth the psychodynamics of stalking in detail.

Dahmer's school grades were now seriously declining owing to his heavy drinking and continuing apathy toward academic and social interactions. His parents hired a private tutor for their son, but this had only limited success. Jeffrey was also regularly seeing his doctor throughout 1976 to 1978. He constantly suffered from 'ragweed hay fever' and was prescribed Kenalog injections to relieve his symptoms. The side effects caused him multiple stomach upsets, headaches and dizziness. He had trouble sleeping. He gained weight. Combined with high alcohol consumption it's a wonder he ever slept at all.

For their part, Lionel and Joyce had enough of their own problems to deal with. They were attending counselling sessions, to try and resolve their differences and save their marriage, which proved unsuccessful. The Dahmers were sliding, inevitably towards divorce.

Divorce

Statistics show that that circa forty-four per cent of marriages will end in divorce. While this may be the best decision for these failed marriages in the long run, the short-term effects can be devastating to everyone involved. Much of the time, it is the children that feel the greatest trauma, and undoubtedly, as will soon become apparent, Jeffrey's parents' divorce affected him and brought him to one of the most dramatic waypoints in his life. All children react differently to divorce, but psychologists have noted that children can react differently according to age. Young children often experience grief when they learn that their parents are separating and become sad and clingy. On the other hand, adolescents like Jeffrey Dahmer often view divorce as a betrayal and pull away from their parents. They can act out, often becoming extremely angry at one or both parents – the result of which can be abusive behaviour such as shouting and name-calling. Or they may withdraw from family contact and into themselves. Adolescents may become less engaged with school, responsibilities and other activities. Grades will often drop, and one may notice a marked increase in truancy. The teenager may increase in dangerous or self-harming behaviour such as binge drinking, using drugs and sexual promiscuity. Unfortunately, studies have shown that adolescents who experience parents' divorce can be affected long into adulthood. Indeed, children of divorced parents can experience a fear of relationships and be reluctant to commit. Many people report having trust issues. These problems may lead to other often pathological problems that can undermine their own relationships. For Jeffrey, his parents' divorce was nothing less than a nuclear explosion.

As the marriage deteriorated, Lionel was at his wits' end. To say that he was terrified of his wife was an understatement – he started stringing trip wires tagged with keys that would rattle if someone approached while he slept. By the time the first legal papers were filed in the Summit County Court of Common Pleas before Judge Richard V. Zurz in late 1977, things had gone from bad to worse.

The proceedings teed off with Lionel filing first. He had discovered that, while Joyce was attending her father's funeral out of state, she had had an affair. The couple had told both boys that any divorce would be an amicable arrangement, but Lionel, perhaps still smarting at his wife's infidelity, decided to get his foot in the legal door first. His attorney sent Joyce a registered letter telling her that she had seven days to pack up her stuff and move out of the marital home. In early 1978, Lionel moved out of the house to stay at the no-nonsense Ohio Motel at 2248 North Cleveland Massillon Road about ten miles away.

The arguing resumed. They fought like cat and dog, threatening each other while the two boys stood meekly by as frightened spectators. Lionel told his boys that their mom was crazy. Fighting hard to control her boiling emotions and appear calm in order to prove him wrong, Joyce told them, 'Your father is a liar. He's a very sick man.' Joyce soon fired back with legal filings and soon both parties were alleging extreme cruelty and gross neglect. She accused him of being over-sexed, which was a bit ripe as it had been she that had been unfaithful. 'As Divorce Action 77-11-4162' grew thicker in its manila folder, there would be repeated references to Joyce's mental condition,' writes Don Davis in his book.[14] Her lawyer declared in one hearing that Mr Dahmer was harassing Joyce because 'he was intent upon driving Mrs Dahmer back to the psychiatrist.' Lionel's attorney countered in an objection citing the 'extensive mental illness of the defendant, Mrs Dahmer'. And the accusations came thick and fast.

The court now ordered that Joyce should undergo a psychological evaluation in Akron, Ohio. To beef things up, Lionel sent the psychologist copious notes as to her mental condition and the history of her addiction to medication. However, he need not have troubled himself. The doctors realised that she had multiple issues during their first session with her. Joyce would stay as an in-patient for a while. The report from the psychologist concluded what Lionel had already known for years. She had refused to share the marital bed yet had told a neighbour that he was sexually 'insatiable'. The report stated that she suffered from 'very severe emotional problems. She is constantly angry, frustrated and demanding in her interpersonal relationships. She insists on interpreting the motives of all those around her and seems to deny anyone's right to discuss her own behaviour as it affects others.' The psychologist then learned that Mrs Dahmer was attending a women's circle at a community mental health centre. Lionel it seems was even now anxious to save their failing marriage and was willing to seek further professional help, but she would have none of it – the reason being that she had found another man.

This was all happening in 1978, the year that Jeffrey was to graduate high school. A few weeks beforehand, one of his teachers watched him sitting close to the school parking lot, drinking several cans of beer. When the teacher threatened to report the matter, Dahmer told him he was experiencing 'a lot of problems at home', and that the school's guidance counsellor was aware of them. There could have been something much darker going on behind the scenes. In 1982, when Jeffrey Dahmer was twenty-two years old, his mother won a restraining order that prohibited her husband from 'molesting or assaulting her or the minor children.' Jeffrey Dahmer would later tell investigators that although he was never abused by his parents, his childhood was 'not happy'. He described his feelings toward both his mother and father as 'mixed or neutral ... the house was in turmoil.'

With all the trouble at home, young Dahmer was increasingly turning to the drink and was becoming dangerously disconnected from just about everything going on around him. He was about to turn eighteen in May. He was nearly always by himself and was now drinking a twelve-pack of beer a day. His eyes were always bloodshot. He was smoking dope and appeared to his teachers as solemn and depressed. This was his senior year and the year of his prom – an event where every young lad should have a date on his arm. Jeffrey, although quite a good-looking guy, was not popular with girls. He'd never looked twice at girls – of course he was gay so why would he? As was to be expected, he didn't want to go to the festivities, but felt pressure to do so. The high school prom is a rite of passage and a tradition. It fell to others to find a date for Jeff. And it proved to be an unmitigated disaster.

For the reader who would like to delve deeper into Jeff's life up until this point, I thoroughly recommend the movie *My Friend Dahmer*. The writer-director, Marc Meyers, has crafted a haunting and evocative look at Dahmer's younger years and the film is based on the critically acclaimed graphic novel of the same name by Jeffrey's classmate, Derf Backderf. The film covers Dahmer's troubled upbringing and childhood and ends with the high school prom.

Finally, and almost at his own wits' end, Judge Kurz found a compromise, and granted the divorce in July 1978. Joyce would get custody of 'the minor child' David, along with $225 a month in support and maintenance, $400 a month in alimony for six years with an additional bung of $125 per month if she attended college. She also got half of the shares that her husband had purchased in PPG stock, and the family's ten-year-old Oldsmobile Cutlass. As Robin Williams once said: 'Ah, yes, divorce…from the Latin word meaning to rip out a man's genitals through his wallet.'

Lionel must have driven away from the courthouse contemplating that their marriage had begun with the two of them wanting to get the best out of each other and ended with them both getting the worst. He had also fought hard for custody of David. David was only twelve in 1978. Though Joyce originally got custody, over the years, circumstances changed, and David eventually chose to live with his father.

The ruling also granted Joyce ownership of part of the house on West Bath Road. Oddly, she agreed to quit any claim over the house and give it to Lionel, on the proviso that when he came up with a hefty $23,500 for her share in it, then and only then it would be all his. Having just turned eighteen, Jeff was legally an adult and thus not subject to such court custodial considerations. In Spring 1978, Joyce made the decision to move out of the family home and stay with members of her own family in Chippewa Falls, Wisconsin. She took David with her but left Jeffrey behind. Lionel was still living at the motel in Ohio. Jeffrey Dahmer was left by his mother, all alone, to fend for himself in an isolated house sitting in deep woods. He later recalled of that time:

> 'Maybe I started shutting down during the divorce proceedings. It was my way of shutting out any painful thoughts, just taking an attitude of not caring or pretending not to care, to save myself the pain of what was going on with the divorce. Maybe it started then. That was effective. It worked.'

A mere five months later forty-two-year-old Lionel married again. Just before Christmas, 1978, he tied the knot with thirty-seven-year-old Shari, herself a divorcee of four years. Joyce took back her maiden name, 'Flint', to erase 'Dahmer' from her name as well as her life. But the acrimony didn't cease. Two years later, Joyce summoned the police to West Bath Road. She claimed that she and her ex-husband had argued again that he had attacked her with angry words and with his hands. Quite what Joyce was doing visiting the house she had left behind is unknown, but the cops quietened her down and reported no injuries. No charges were ever filed.

Jeffrey Dahmer graduated from high school in June 1978. Just three weeks later he would commit his first murder.

Crossing the Rubicon – Steven Mark Hicks

'Experience is the teacher of all things.'

Julius Caesar

Did you know that the month of July is named after Julius Caesar? Hey, guess what...? I didn't know this either until I watched a Netflix documentary about the history of the Roman Empire. So I looked up my birthday month – April – and I couldn't find any reference to a high-ranking Roman called April being in Rome at that time – nor anywhere else come to that. In fact, I discovered that the root of April comes from Latin 'Aprilis': derived from the Latin *'aperire'* meaning 'to open' which could be something to do with opening doors or the blossoming of flowers and trees. See, one learns something new every day and why not, I say?

When Julius crossed the Rubicon River on 10 January 49 BC to precipitate the Roman Civil War, he knew that there could be no turning back. This also applied to Dahmer. That June of 1978, was when he had his crossing the Rubicon moment, and opened the door to committing homicide. He made his first kill. So far, he had merely been dabbling in dissection and having lurid, sexually-driven fantasies about what he would like to do with a young man. Now, just like April flowers blossom, so did Jeffrey – into a stone-cold killer.

Jeffrey had been abandoned by both his parents to fend for himself. He was left to his own devices for days on end. There were woods all around his home which shielded him from prying eyes and made disposal of a body an easy task. It could be right to say that without the toxic combination of his emotions, murder might have remained in the realms of fantasy. But the shame of his repressed homosexuality, rage, self-pity, resentment, loneliness *and* excess alcohol combined with opportunity to turn fantasy into murderous reality. Another waypoint was imminent. In previous writings I have mentioned the 'Murder Road' – the tragic train of events that lead to a crossroads where two lives meet, and one life is tragically and brutally brought to an end.

Eighteen-year-old Dahmer's first victim was a hitchhiker called Steven Mark Hicks, whom he spotted thumbing along a road in Summit County on 18 June 1978. Unlike Dahmer, Steve had a lot of buddies. It was just a few days before his nineteenth birthday when he had gone out for a day of summertime fun at a rock concert in Chippewa Lake Park. Hitchhiking along Ohio Route 224, he was picked up by a group of friends who took him to the park in Medina County. They spent the day together then the group left with him promising to meet them later at an old landing strip near Lockwood

Corners. 'I will hitch there,' he told them. 'It's my dad's birthday. I need to give him a present. We are having a family party this evening.' Apart from Dahmer, nobody saw Steven Hicks alive again.

After his arrest in July 1991, for multiple homicides, Jeff told Police Lt. Richard Munsey about what happened to Steven. Dahmer was driving an Oldsmobile Cutlass when he spotted the handsome youth thumbing for a ride on Cleveland-Massillon Road. Steven was wearing blue jeans, a necklace chain with a red cross on it, and blue tennis shoes. Instantly Dahmer's priapic predatory sexual desires were aroused. 'I wish I hadn't stopped and turned around and picked him up,' he later told police, 'that's when the nightmare became a reality.'

He lured Steven to his home on the pretext of the two of them drinking alcohol together and Hicks agreed to the offer. After several hours of listening to music and drinking, Hicks 'wanted to leave and [I] didn't want him to,' said Dahmer. Hicks was not gay and had bluntly rejected his host's sexual advances. They argued and Jeffrey struck Steven twice from behind with a dumbbell – given to him by his father – as the youth sat on a chair in front of the bookcase in the den. When Steven fell unconscious Dahmer throttled him to death with the bar of the dumbbell. He then stripped Steven's body of his clothes before masturbating over the corpse.

During his confession, Dahmer vividly and without emotion recalled how he went about getting rid of Steven Hicks once he had killed him. He had dragged the body around to the crawl space beneath the house. Remember his fascination watching his father removing animal bones from beneath the house – even aged four the sound of the dry bones had given him a thrill. He had used a long knife and the knowledge he'd gained in slicing up animals to dismember Steven, exerting final control over the new friend he had just met. We can see now how this progression from fantasy had eventually turned into murder most foul. There could be no turning back. The Rubicon had been crossed.

Opportunist murderers, such as Dahmer, act upon impulse. The entrapment of a victim comes easy to them, the kill is easy too. Disposing of a corpse is another, more complicated matter entirely. In this disgusting case, the various parts of Steven's remains were stuffed into plastic garbage bags and hidden in the crawl space. In the heat of the summer, flesh and organs would have started to quickly decompose. The sickly-sweet nauseating stench of decomposition is instantly, vomit-retchingly noticeable. Cops who have discovered such human remains in a home often have to burn their clothes because the odour sticks to the fabric as the remains bake and stew in their bodily juices – in this case the plastic bags began to fill with gas.

For Dahmer, this situation was becoming ever riskier for him. Yes, he was alone in the house, but his father might call unannounced at any time. Shit would happen if neighbours and nosy kids came banging on the door. Of course they would know he was at home – his fucking car is parked in the driveway. Can you see Jeff now…? Half-drunk and sweating like a pig. His mind befuddled with a throbbing hangover.

Then a light switched on inside his brain. He reasoned that the most sensible thing was to bury the remains on nearby land. The ground around the house was rocky so the grave that Jeff dug was shallow. This was a bad move by Jeff because foraging animals can smell decomposing flesh from miles away. Can you imagine all those little critters out there sniffing the air and thinking, 'Hey guys, dinner is served'!

That night – a sleepless one no doubt – Dahmer started to panic. What if local kids playing in the woods noticed something different? When he was a kid he had known every twig, branch and root and had prided himself that he could flyspeck-spot anything that had been changed. For God's sake, that shallow grave might stand out. So he dug Steven's remains up and was presently back to square one. Dahmer unearthed the rotting remains and pared the flesh from the bones before dissolving it in acid. Then he flushed the solution down the toilet. He crushed Steven's bones to fragments with a sledgehammer and scattered them in woodland behind the house and over the property lines of 4480 West Bath Road, 4410 West Bath Road and 4464 Bath Road – the last address being the property belonging to Elmer and Georgia Scharenberg.

When reported missing by his parents, Steven Hicks was described as: 'Born 27 June 1959; weight 150 pounds; height 5'10"; brown eyes; brown hair; scar on forearm; birthmark the size of a dime on back; dental records available.'

It transpired during later interviews after his arrest that the shallow grave was not the first resting place Dahmer thought of for Steven and that there was a moment in the early hours of the morning where Jeffrey Dahmer could have been stopped in his tracks. What follows is verbatim from an FBI document file number 7-MW-26057-83 dated September 1992:[15]

> 'Dahmer stated that he had sex with the dead body [Stephen Hicks]. Dahmer further advised that later that night, during the early morning hours, he had the Hicks body cut up and placed in a trash bag and was driving down the street when a patrol car stopped him. Dahmer stated that two police officers then ordered him out of the car, and they shined their flashlights in his car and saw the garbage bag, and asked Dahmer what was in the bag and what the terrible smell was, and Dahmer told them that he was just bringing some old garbage to the city dump. Dahmer stated that the officers never looked in the bag and just gave him a ticket for driving left of the centre.
>
> Dahmer stated that this incident frightened him, and he fully expected to have been caught. Dahmer stated that he did not kill again for nearly ten years.'

So, what was Jeffrey's true motive behind his first kill? I suggest that one can take his claim that he didn't want Steven to leave him – as a living person – with a pinch of salt. Without wishing to be obtuse, Steven *did* leave the house – in bits. Some bone fragments were later found by police conducting a lengthy fingertip search of the entire property and adjacent woodland. It seems far more probable that he'd invited Hicks to the house with every intention of killing him and thus fulfilling his earlier fantasy about the jogger. What emerged was his sick, psychopathological need to keep *parts* of his victim close by.

The murder of Steven Hicks must have had a crystalising effect on Dahmer's sexual inclinations. He was no longer just a misunderstood loner – he was a killer and potentially even more of an outcast from society. Did he wake up the next morning wishing it had all been a nightmare? If so, he had the means of forgetfulness ready to hand – alcohol. One can imagine Jeffrey as he crawled out of his bed and stood over the body of Steven Hicks, cleaned his spectacles, scratched the top of his head, then thought dumbly: 'Ummm, now what the *fuck* do I do now?'

Six weeks after the homicide of Steven Hicks, Lionel Dahmer returned to 4480 Bath Road with his fiancée, Shari to discover Jeffrey living there alone. 'He had a dead look in his eyes. He looked extremely sad,' recalled Lionel. Shari remembers that, 'Jeff was wandering aimlessly about the house. He looked uncomfortable. His mother had moved out … he was torn between two characters. He was a lost child. What most people wanted to do was mother him. He needed love. He needed attention.'

At his father's insistence, Jeffrey enrolled at Ohio State University OSU in August, hoping to major in business studies. But alcoholism had destroyed the will to work. He would take alcohol into class and get drunk as he listened to his tutors. Lionel paid him a surprise visit one day and, to his shock, found Jeff's room strewn with empty liquor bottles. Jeff was even selling his own blood at a blood bank to earn money to buy booze. He received failing grades in Introduction to Anthropology and Administrative Science. The only course Jeffrey was successful at was Riflery, for which he received a B grade. When $120, a radio and a watch disappeared from a college dorm, he was questioned by the campus police, but no charge was made. One fellow student saw Jeff lying drunk in the street in Columbus and felt that nothing could save him from self-destruction. Despite his father having paid in advance for a second term, Jeffrey dropped out of university after just three months.

Jeffrey Dahmer was now only a bottle of the hard stuff away from skid row.

Mind Control

'I must confess to you; I'm giving very serious thought to eating your wife.'

Dr Hannibal Lecter to Inspector Rinaldo
(Giancarlo Giannini) Pazzi, *Hannibal* (2001)

Before we get even deeper into more blood and guts, it is fair to say that we should realise that most dyed-in-the-wool psychopaths don't have a conscience the same way we 'normal' people do. Where there should be empathy towards their fellow humans there is a black hole. Moreover, at the heart of every sexual psychopath is the overwhelming need to control other people's minds using guile, intimidation and even resorting to threats of physical violence to get their own way. Impenitent, demeaning, hard-wired for amorality and incapable of showing any regret, they are unashamedly wicked to their very cores. They are master manipulators. If they weep, they cry crocodile tears. I have interviewed several serial killers who have exhibited this fake regret, but they are only sobbing over the incarceration they have found themselves in. Oh, boy, and wouldn't you if you were on The Green Mile, just a short stumbling walk to 'Ole Sparky'?

Another thing I have learned through my experiences with these monsters is that most of them are extreme narcissists. They have a grandiose sense of their own importance and live in their own fantasy worlds that support their own delusions of grandeur – existences where elephants fly, lead balls bounce and fairies reign supreme. They are inclined to seek constant praise and admiration. They also have a keen sense of entitlement, and they will exploit others without guilt or shame.

The noun 'narcissism' gets bounced around a lot in our selfie-obsessed celebrity-driven culture; used often to describe someone who seems excessively vain or full of themselves. It's often used to describe the last President, Donald J. Trump. Well, he is akin to Marmite in that you either love him or you don't. However, in psychological terms, narcissism does not mean self-love – at least not of the genuine sort. It is more accurate to say that people with narcissistic personality disorders are in love with an idealised, grandiose image of themselves. They are in love with this inflated self-image precisely because it allows them to avoid deep feelings of insecurity. But propping up their delusions of grandeur takes a lot of work and that is where dysfunctional attitudes and behaviours come into play.

Narcissistic personality disorder (NPD) involves a pattern of self-centred, arrogant thinking and behaviour, a lack of empathy and consideration for other people and an excessive need for admiration. In some ways,

Joyce Dahmer fitted this mindset. Where the sociopathy/psychopathy comes into play is that people with NPD are extremely resistant to changing their behaviour, even when it is causing them problems. And there is a reason for this: the narcissist's tendency is to put the blame for their own faults onto others. This 'blame dumping' can be aimed in the direction of a partner, work colleagues, police, an inadequate lawyer, the courts or even the system itself. This 'psychological projection' works as a defence mechanism which allows the ego to defend itself against unconscious impulses or qualities (both positive and negative) by denying their existence in themselves or by attributing them to others. This projection tends to come to the fore in normal people at times of crisis, but it is more commonly found in narcissistic personality disorder or borderline personality disorder. Interview any convicted felon, and he, or she, is bound to try and shift the blame onto someone or something else, in a 'Not me, Guv!' sort of way.

I recall interviewing the sado-sexual serial killer Harvey 'Harv The Hammer' Carignan at the Minnesota Correctional Facility (MCF) many years ago. Known as 'The Want-Ad Killer', Harvey was only convicted of three murders but suspected of around fifty. He was a giant of a man, yet softly-spoken in a grandfatherly sort of way. We sat across a table from each other while, without a shred of remorse, he blithely blamed his victims for their own rapes and murders. He claimed that he had merely offered them a ride and then they falsely accused him of raping them so, 'I was forced to kill them, or I'd be charged for something I hadn't done.' When I put it to him that I might understand this happening once or twice 'but *not dozens* of times,' and reminded him that he had not only killed his victims but had 'beaten their heads into a pulp,' he smirked. 'Well, that was their problem,' he said, adding, 'Fuck them, they played mind games with my head, so I smashed their heads in. Get it?'

One of the fascinating things about Jeff Dahmer was that he never tried to dump the blame onto anyone or anything else. He accepted what he did was wrong, and he understood that he would need to be punished. In this regard he was a very unusual psychopath – quite unique as far as I can tell – so-much-so that even post-mortem he is worthy of in-depth study.

More often than not, the media erroneously and sensationally label serial killers such as Jeff Dahmer as being 'mad', when in the strict legal sense, they are not. Yes, the 'Milwaukee Cannibal' was a monster by any sane person's reasoning: he drugged or clubbed unconscious innocent young men and strangled them to death. He dismembered their corpses, sometimes cooking and eating their body parts or keeping artefacts such as their skulls, as painted keepsakes or, as some will say, 'trophies'. As we shall see later in this book, a determined effort was made by his defence-appointed psychiatrist, the eminent Frederick S. Berlin, Director of the Sexual Disorders Clinic at John Hopkins University in Baltimore, who told the trial court as part of the Defence's efforts to have Dahmer committed to a mental institution rather than be incarcerated in a prison: 'Here's a man [Dahmer] who is preoccupied with these [evil] thoughts until it becomes a way of life for him. I think he's afflicted with these recurrent urges and fantasies, a terrible sickness ... a cancer of the mind. If this isn't a mental illness, from my point of view, I don't what is.'

In many respects Fred Berlin *is* correct, but there are several fundamental problems with this argument. One being that Dahmer had been diagnosed as a sexual psychopath for which there is no known cure. Once a psychopath always a psychopath, so being incarcerated in a cushy asylum instead of a mainstream penitentiary wouldn't have changed anything at all. If I were to be glib, I vividly recall death row warden Neil Hodges, as he pointed, unsmiling, to the lethal injection gurney at The Walls Prison in Huntsville, tell me that there the only cure for psychopathy was to 'Strap them down on there and that cures everything.' An additional problem was that if Dahmer *had* been committed to a mental institution, there was a chance that, at some time in the future he might have been released back into society. Dahmer was not 'mad' or 'insane' in the eyes of the law. He knew what he was doing was wrong and he was crafty enough to be able to cover his tracks for years. He was cunning and manipulative to a fault. There also remains the fact that 'The Milwaukee Cannibal' caused immeasurable heartbreak to his victims' next-of-kin. There will be those amongst them who might have suggested – even demanded – that he should have been hung, drawn and quartered. God bless them – they are, of course, entitled to their own opinion. I am sure I would want that if one of my own children had been murdered so brutally and their remains treated so horrifically – wouldn't you?

Medical Specialist in the Army

'Count the brave, count the true, who have fought to victory.
We're the army and proud of our name.'

US Army song

With his college hopes in tatters and no other opportunities for work now open to him, Jeff's next waypoint again came about at a frustrated Lionel's urging. According to FBI files, on 29 December 1978 Jeffrey Dahmer (Social Security card number: 284-60-5333) enlisted in the US Army with a grade PVT E-1. His initial intention was to become a military police officer; and agreed that he would be enlisting for a period of three years. At first, he went to the Military Police School at Fort McClellan, Alabama, for an eight-week course which, to no one's surprise, he failed to complete. On 11 May 1979, he was sent for another eight-week course at the Army Hospital School, Fort Sam Houston, San Antonio, Texas. Known as 'Fort Sam', the installation's mission includes serving as the Command HQ for the United

States Army North, United States Army South, the Army Medical Command (MEDCOM) headquarters, and the Army Medical Department AMEDD Center and School.

One might have thought that there was a very strict physical and psychological examination before one is selected for training in the US forces. Not so, it appears in Dahmer's case. Perhaps during his interviews he had mentioned an interest in bones and bodies, who knows? But if *anyone* living in the US was *totally unsuitable* for serving in the armed forces it was Jeffrey Dahmer – period!

On 13 June 1979, Dahmer was assigned to Headquarters Company, 26th Armor Division, Second Battalion, 68th Armor in Baumholder, West Germany. He would serve here as a combat medic until 24 March 1981. His military file shows that: 'Dahmer was a sharpshooter with the M-16 weapon and a marksman with the .45 pistol.' He was regarded by his fellow soldiers as hard to figure out, 'bright ... always able to devour books as well as brews ... an oddball who also wore his military uniform with pride.' Some of his favourite books were children's classic fairy tales of trolls and goblins. He was into the Iron Maiden rock band – heavy metal was his thing. Although booze was banned, Jeffrey always found a way around that problem. He would drink himself stupid. His fellow peers started to recognise that he had a Dr Jekyll and Mr Hyde personality. When he was not in the drink he was happy, friendly and able to joke around – doing an imitation of W.C. Fields to get a few laughs. When he was drunk as the proverbial skunk, he became obnoxious and lost what little control that he had left. It was during these times that his pals saw his face turn into an empty mask. His eyes would become glazed, he would become surly and prone to shouting and arguments which often included racist insults.

An article fifteen (non-judicial punishment) was filed by the commander of the base in Germany to investigate Dahmer's conduct. It makes for grim reading:

> 'It was reported that Dahmer, having knowledge of a verbal order issued by a ranking officer in which it was his duty to obey, did, at Baumholder, Germany, on or about May 30 1980, wrongfully fail to obey the same by having hard liquor in his billits [*sic*]. It was also alleged that he behaved with disrespect towards his ranking superior commissioned officer by saying to him in effect "I'm not going to fucking do it."

> 'It was further alleged that, on this same date, he was drunk and disorderly in his quarters and that this was in violation of military rules. The punishment imposed was that he was reduced to the grade of E-14, suspended until September 5, 1980, with a forfeiture of $100.00 per month for two months, and fifteen days extra duty.

> 'Dahmer's medical records indicate that on a self-reported medical checklist, he indicated

that he does wear glasses, and has been treated for hay fever and a ruptured hernia in the past.

'According to the records of informal counselling sessions, DAHMER was reprimanded on the following occasions:

'August 8, 1980, he was counselled due to the fact that he was caught going through BEQ (Bachelor Enlisted Quarters) looking into a refrigerator for food and that he had no business being in the BEQ, and that that behaviour would not be tolerated.

'On August 11, 1980, he was counselled on an incident which occurred on August 2, 1980, when he was picked up by the Military Police for being under the influence of alcohol and [told] that this behaviour would not be tolerated.

'On September 2 1980, he was counselled on an incident that occurred in the barracks on August 30, 1980, on the fact that his stereo was too loud and after being told by a commanding officer to turn it down, if he did not and if this incident occurred again, the radio would be taken away from him for thirty days.

'On or around December 8, 1980, Dahmer arrived for work four minutes late and, upon his arrival, was so intoxicated he could not even stand up.

'On December 22, 1980, he was written up for being drunk and disorderly during the previous weekend on several occasions.

'On December 22, 1980, he arrived on duty heavily intoxicated and at that time the recommendation was for maximum judicial punishment; on December 23, 1980, he was counselled because he had failed to perform a duty that was assigned to him, and he was again intoxicated.

'On March 7, 1981, Dahmer reported for formation in improper uniform and was sent back to his room to get in proper material.'

The FBI, later, further confirm:

'Dahmer was the subject of numerous actions on the part of the military for alcohol abuse. His file reflects numerous periods of counselling by enlisted personnel and officers regarding his behaviour and actions that were the result of his alcohol abuse.

'Notations in his military file reflect counselling by (name redacted) his platoon sergeant, on 8/8/80, 6/11/80, 9/2/80, 12/8/80, 12/23/80, 3/7/81, and 3/9/81.

'Dahmer was enrolled in an alcoholic rehabilitation programme on 2/5/81 but stated that he was not willing to control his alcohol intake.'

During his first year of service, Jeff Dahmer was reported to be an 'average or slightly above average soldier.' However, more importantly, two soldiers later attested to having been sexually assaulted by Dahmer. One soldier claimed he was drugged, then raped by Dahmer inside an armoured personnel carrier. The other claimed he had been repeatedly raped over a lengthy period by Dahmer.

It might come as no shock to the reader to learn that sexual assaults have been a problem in the US military for years. The second victim that Dahmer assaulted, Billy Joe Capshaw, was just seventeen years old and was raped so many times over so many months it became one long brutal blur. Capshaw was so traumatised that, when he arrived back home in Arkansas, he was unable to speak of his experiences or socialise in way. He would eventually tell the *Independent*: 'I could not say I was raped; I could not do that to my daddy. He fought in the Pacific. He would have thought that I was a faggot.' Capshaw went through twenty-six years in therapy due to the terror Dahmer subjected him to. This disgusting systemic type of sexual abuse within the army was confirmed by the US Defense Department in May 2013, when they estimated that a staggering 26,000 members of the military had suffered unwanted sexual contact in 2012 – which was a forty per cent jump over the previous two years. Whilst they have at least acknowledged the problem, the US Army needs to buck itself up, if you care to ask me.

In his later interviews with police, Dahmer recalled that he had once been approached by a master sergeant in the mess hall of Landstuhl Hospital at the German army base. 'He had his own apartment,' said Dahmer, 'and one night I was drinking in the local NCO club, and he said to me that he had a party going on back at his place. He asked me if I wanted to go back, and I said "Sure". And we went back. Turned out there was nobody in the apartment, just him. And he lights up this bowl of hash, smoked some hash, drank some beer. And he goes [and] takes his shower, comes back and tries to get me to hop in bed with him. I said, "No thanks". So, I just go walking out, staggering after that hash. That was the first time I'd been approached.'

Due to his alcohol abuse, PFC Dahmer's performance deteriorated, and, in March 1981, he was deemed unsuitable for life in the military – the army wanted rid of him. Somewhat remarkably he received an honourable discharge as his superiors did not believe that any problems Dahmer had in the army would be applicable to civilian life. Oh, boy. Did they get that *wrong*.

On 24 March 1981, Jeffrey was sent to Fort Jackson, South Carolina, for debriefing and provided with a plane ticket to travel anywhere in the US. He was formally discharged two days afterwards, telling a colleague, 'One day you'll hear of me again.' However, he felt he could not return home to face his father in disgrace, so he opted to travel to Miami Beach, Florida, because he was 'tired of the cold' and wanted to attempt to live by his 'own means.'

After his discharge from the army and upon his arrival on Florida's 'Gold Coast', Jeffrey found employment at the Sunshine Subs delicatessen. He rented a nearby hotel room along Collins Avenue in Bimini, which had a view over the beach, but spent most of his wages on alcohol. Sunshine Subs was a family run business, the supervisor being sixty-five-year-old Ken Houles. One of Jeff's colleagues there was a young British woman in her mid to late twenties who was working illegally as she didn't have a Green Card. 'She was a nice girl, but we didn't speak much,' he later told police as something as an afterthought.

Dahmer wasn't actually flat broke when he arrived in Florida. He still had about $1,000 in army pay in his bank account. He claimed that he was mugged of $100.00 by three men on the beach when he was so drunk that he was as 'sick as a dog.' But with his drinking habit to fund, Dahmer had almost frittered the money away and soon found himself facing eviction from the hotel for non-payment of rent. Eventually he was forced to spend his nights on the beach sleeping under mangroves, taking a shower maybe once or twice a week as he continued to work at the deli. Finally, he became so desperate he phoned his father to ask him if he could return to Ohio in the September of that year. Lionel Dahmer acceded to his son's request.

For Jeffrey this would be his 'Last Chance Saloon'.

The 'Last Chance Saloon'

'To lose patience is to lose the battle.'

Mahatma Gandhi (1869-1948)

Despite any deep-felt regrets that Lionel Dahmer may have harboured as to how he'd raised his son, at least he kept stepping up to the plate to help him out. Joyce had skedaddled over the horizon, washing her hands of Jeffrey pretty much for good. It might seem that I have given Joyce a rough hearing thus far, however, she did go on to do good things. Later she went to California, where she worked as a caseworker then manager for the Central Valley AIDS Team. In 1996, she founded The Living Room: a community centre for HIV positive individuals. Her work with those affected by HIV and AIDS meant she was adored by many. Joyce Flint passed away, dying of breast cancer on 27 November 2000 aged sixty-four.

Upon learning that his son had been thrown out of the army and was now homeless, Lionel invited Jeffrey to

120

come and live with him and his wife in their smart home in Granger Township, Medina County, a stone's throw from West Allis. But his son was no longer the lad Lionel had raised by a long chalk. Unknown to Lionel, by this time Jeff had killed Steven Hicks, he had raped fellow soldiers and inflicted violence on them. He had also walked the red-light streets of K-Town and had drifted on the 'Gold Coast' of Florida, soaked up the sun and got himself smashed on Grasshoppers. The Granger Township (population circa 4,000) must have amounted to a sleepy backwater.

Initially, however, this arrangement started out quite well. Jeff Dahmer insisted that he help his stepmother with chores around the place to occupy his time while he sought employment. However, he continued to drink heavily. His father remembers that Jeff would be out all hours, getting drunk at bars until closing time, getting into fights and even forgetting where he had parked the family car. On 7 October 1981 – arrogant and spoiling for trouble, just weeks after his return to Granger Township – he was arrested for drunk and disorderly conduct after carrying an open bottle of vodka into the lounge of the Bath Township Ramada Inn. He was fined $60 and received a suspended ten-day jail sentence.

With the patience of a saint, Lionel tried to wean his son off alcohol. Sadly, this failed. After the incident at the Ramada Inn, Jeffrey was packed off to live with his grandmother, Catherine Jemima Hughes (1904-1992) who lived in a detached house at 2357 South 57th Street, West Allis. Jeff Dahmer had now arrived at another decisive waypoint in his life. We must ask ourselves honestly though, if the US Army with its strict discipline and demanding work ethic couldn't straighten the young man out what chance would a frail but determined old lady have? Can we say, 'Not a snowball's chance in hell'?

West Allis is allegedly a nice place to live; it's a city in Milwaukee County (population circa 60,000). There are many green parks. Situated about a ten-minute drive east is Milwaukee Bay. Based on current FBI crime data, West Allis is *not* one of the safest communities in America. In fact, West Allis has a crime rate that is higher than ninety-five per cent of all the state's cities and towns of all sizes.

Grandma Catherine was a church-goer and was seriously old school with all-American, traditional values. She'd married Herbert Walter Dahmer in 1933. Can you imagine Catherine welcoming her grandson on the stoop of her pretty two-storey house with a white siding over tan block with red shutters on the three top front windows under a rust-coloured shingled roof. She might be wearing a crisp white blouse and could have just baked apple pie. Out front there is a manicured lawn and a tree. The entire street is lined with trees, similar homes belonging to neighbours. It's the sort of street which we see in the early American TV commercials with one or two 'Futuramatic' Oldsmobiles crawling past and rosy-cheeked kids eating Tootsie Rolls. A dear old dear, was Grandma Catherine. Like her son, Lionel, she had the patience of a saint too and she'd need all of it over the coming days and weeks. Furthermore, she was the only member of the family – and probably the entire world – to whom Jeffrey displayed any affection. So Lionel hoped and prayed on bended knees that her influence, and the change of scenery, might inspire his son to refrain from alcohol, find a job, and live responsibly.

Jeffrey's living arrangements with Grandma were initially harmonious. He accompanied her to church, willingly undertook chores and he was the model grandson... *initially*. Although he did continue to drink and smoke, he largely adhered by her fairly strict house rules. Yet, this new stage in his life brought some positive results and, in early 1982, he found a job as a phlebotomist at the Milwaukee Blood Plasma Centre – perfect employment for an emerging cannibal, one might think. Count Dracula would have been well at home there too. But there were more dark clouds on the horizon.

There are many varying accounts and dates attributed to Dahmer's early criminal antecedents, but I have used police and FBI files to give us more accurate details. According to Milwaukee Police Department records, on 8 August, 1982, at the Wisconsin State Fair Park, Dahmer was arrested for disorderly conduct. A month later, on 8 September 1982, he was again arrested; this time on a charge of lewd and lascivious behaviour after he committed indecent exposure to a crowd of no less than twenty-five women and children. He was placed on probation for one year and fined $50 plus court costs. His employers at the blood plasma centre sacked him. He remained out of work for over two years, during which he lived upon whatever money Grandma gave him.

On 14 January 1985, Dahmer was hired as a 'mixer' in the Ambrosia Chocolate Company with its looming factory on North Fifth Street, just to the northwest of the Bradley Centre. The company had been formed in 1894 by Otto J. Schoenleber and his products gained a reputation as 'The Food of the Gods' aka 'Ambrosia', and over the next three decades established itself as a leader in selling penny sweets and candies. His pay cheque was $8.25 per hour. He worked mixing vats of chocolate from 11 p.m. to 7 a.m., six nights a week.

According to Dahmer, shortly after starting work at the factory, he was propositioned by a man while sitting reading in the West Allis Public Library. The stranger, says Dahmer, threw him a note offering to perform fellatio upon him. Although Dahmer did not respond to this proposition, he says that this incident stirred, once again, in his mind the fantasies of control and dominance he'd developed then nurtured as a teenager. So, as well as mixing chocolate, Dahmer was soon also mixing in Milwaukee's gay bars, where he became known as a monosyllabic loner. Looking back through the statements Dahmer later gave to police, this alleged West Allis Library incident has identical echoes of the master sergeant whom Jeffrey claimed propositioned him in the NCO's bar, in Germany. That a lowly PFC would be allowed to drink in a senior officer's bar is ludicrous as any British warrant officer, or American senior non-commissioned rank, will testify. Furthermore, elsewhere in Dahmer's statements, he claimed a similar incident had occurred while he was living and working in Florida. He alleged that a man tried to pick him up while he browsed in a mall bookstore. The man passed him a note offering fellatio then followed Dahmer around until he told the man to 'fuck off'. When asked by the investigator to provide more details, Dahmer gave two different locations, dates and even cities. Therefore, I think that we can take the West Allis Library yarn with a pinch of salt.

The Club Milwaukee Baths first opened in 1974 as a franchise of the then-popular national Club Bath Chain. Its entrance was situated in an alleyway just north of Wisconsin Avenue, a block from the Central Library. For some time in the middle to late 1970s this club was one of the focal points of the gay men's community in the area. By the late 1970s, with several other gay men's baths also opening in Milwaukee, these establishments had reached critical mass and had attracted the attention of the police department. In 1979, several violent raids on bathhouses were launched by the Milwaukee PD, led by its vehemently anti-gay Chief of Police Harold Breier. These raids resulted in dozens of arrests, and angry street protests by the gay community and their supporters. When the AIDS pandemic arrived several years later, it sounded the death knell for most of the bathhouses and they were closed down.

But it was here in the mid-eighties that Jeffrey Dahmer found himself in his element. He later described the bathhouses as being 'relaxing places.' It was here that he had sexual encounters but found that he became frustrated at his partners' moving about. Before finding live sexual partners, Jeffrey had stolen a male mannequin from a store which he briefly and unsuccessfully used for sexual gratification until an intractably confused Grandma discovered the item stowed in a closet and demanded, much to his chagrin, that he discard it. 'I trained myself to view people as objects of pleasure instead of people,' he told police after his arrest.

Regular patrons of the scene soon observed that Dahmer had another sinister habit. From around 1986, it was noticed that when Jeffrey engaged fellow customers in conversation with the offer of a drink, his companions often ended up in very drunk states. Almost as if Dahmer wanted them to be in a vulnerable state and yet his intention, he said, was 'clearly not to commit rape.' But when one of his drinking companions ended up unconscious in hospital, the owner of the Club Milwaukee Bath was told about it and Jeffrey was barred. Jeff began using hotel rooms for his sexual encounters so he could continue.

So we must understand that, at this stage in Dahmer's criminal narrative, he was practising, developing and learning what worked when selecting someone to use then abuse. He was experimenting and gaining confidence. Like so many emerging serial killers, they learn their deadly trade through trial and error. Although he had killed once previously, he was still what one might call a novice, a 'homicidal undergraduate' if you will.

Steven 'Steve' Walter Tuomi

'I have sewed sackcloth over my skin and thrust my horn in the dust.'

Job 16:15

On 8 September 1986, two twelve-year-old boys, Richard Kohn and John Ostland, reported to police that Dahmer had exposed himself to them while masturbating by a lake at Kinnickinnic River Parkway. Dahmer alleged that he had merely been urinating. The court didn't believe him, so he was sentenced to a year on probation, and, with apparent sincerity, promised his probation officers, 'I'll never go down to the woods again.'

As we have already noted, psychopaths can be extremely convincing. Judges and probation officials have belatedly noted that Dahmer had had a highly convincing manner of expressing sorrow or regret for having done something wrong. Yet, whenever Dahmer apologised for his sins, he was actually sticking two fingers up to the criminal justice system – genuine, watery-eyed contrition was the last thing on his warped mind.

During the probation, he had to undergo mandatory psychotherapy for sexual deviance and impulse control under the guidance of Dr Evelyn Rosen. Rosen utilised the MCMI (Millon Clinical Multiaxial Inventory) assessment to diagnose Dahmer. The test is a tool used to give mental health professionals insights into their patient's personality and psychopathology. It can be used to identify anxiety issues, bipolar disorders, substance abuse issues, schizophrenia, depression and other conditions. The patient must circle a number of statements which best describe themselves and their state of mind.

Dahmer circled the following:

- 'Lately I've begun to feel lonely and empty.'
- 'Ideas keep turning over and over in my mind and they won't go away.'
- 'Looking back on my life, I know I have made others suffer as much as I have suffered.'
- 'I keep having strange thoughts I wish I could get rid of.'

Dr Rosen reported that Dahmer was uncooperative during his sessions with her, remaining silent and even keeping his back to her. However, it has also been speculated that his lack of cooperation was exacerbated by Dr Rosen's approach, which has been described as 'blatant and habitual nagging.' Dahmer was also sent for a session with clinician Kathy Boese at the University of Wisconsin, and this was said to have gone much more smoothly. The clinic's battery of tests concluded that Dahmer was an articulate individual, but he showed little emotion and had 'exceptionally slow' emotional responses. The report stated that 'He resents being told what to do by others and is easily disappointed and hurt ... Dahmer had unrealistic expectations for himself and was not in touch with reality.'

Dahmer's probation period ended on 9 September 1987, and he was quick out of the starting blocks. A year of good behaviour and professional assessment had done nothing to alleviate his psychological problems. On the contrary, the months of restricted sexual deviancy, being under the control of the probation service while living with a strictly moral grandmother had built up resentment and frustration in Jeffrey Dahmer. Six days after his probation ended, with this sexual hunger nagging away like a worm eating into his mind, he exploded into murder most foul.

By mid-September 1987, Dahmer, now aged twenty-eight and free of any legally-binding restrictions, was once again drinking in a gay haunt – a joint called Club 219 found at 219 S. 2nd Street, Milwaukee. It was here that he met handsome twenty-four-year-old Steven Tuomi. They agreed payment in exchange for sex and quickly adjourned to the Ambassador Hotel on Milwaukee Avenue, where they took a room costing $48.88 for the night – Dahmer paying the bill. Tuomi was killed that night.

In his statements later made to Milwaukee Detectives Dennis Murphy and Patrick Kennedy in the presence of his attorney, Wendy Patrickus, Dahmer, who had an excellent memory, claimed that the murder took place, 'about a week before Thanksgiving', which fell on Thursday, 26 November 1987 – meaning that this homicide was committed much later than is generally accepted. I say that he'd first met Tuomi on Tuesday 15 September and they agreed to meet up again, which they did about a week before Thanksgiving – say between 18 to 20 September. This is confirmed by the fact that Dahmer had pre-booked the room at the Ambassador Hotel for the weekend night, and that as he claims 'I had previously prepared sleeping pills in a glass by breaking them down to a powdery form and leaving this form in the glass. When we arrived back at the hotel I gave him a rum and coke with the sleeping potion, and he passed out almost immediately.'

Tuomi hailed from the tiny Michigan township of Ontonagon (population circa 2,500) at the mouth of the Ontonagon River on Lake Superior – outstanding natural beauty all sitting nicely between the Firesteel River and the Porcupine Mountains. Yet, Steven Tuomi wanted more than Ontonagon could offer. Like so many young lads he thought that life would be more exciting in a big city. Milwaukee seemed his best bet, so off he went, finding work as a short-order cook and lodgings on Cass Street on the lower east side. Little did he know that soon he would be butchered like a pig.

Nonetheless, this weekend night with Dahmer was purely a one-off 'client & sex partner' deal. Jeff would later claim that they drank themselves into a stupor and that, when he woke up, 'Tuomi was beneath, dead with blood coming from his mouth and strangulation marks around his throat ... his face was crushed in and black and blue with bruises. He was all bloody ... I think that I may have murdered him.' He would also tell police that he had no recollection of what had happened although he admitted 'my fists and forearm were extensively bruised.'

Jeffrey was now in a bit of a fix. The logistical matter of disposing of Stephen Hicks's body had been relatively easy despite a few glitches. He had been alone in his parents' home set deep in woodland. He had time, space and privacy to carry out the dismemberment and to dispose of Hicks. Now Dahmer found himself in a hotel room with Tuomi's blood-spattered corpse. Room service would be needing to do a tidy-up. Check-out time was approaching. Jeff was up the proverbial 'Shit's Creek'. He booked the room for a second night and hung a 'Do Not Disturb' tag on the doorknob – he had work to do. Jeff decided that he needed to buy a suitcase as soon as possible. He went to the Grand Avenue Mall, where he purchased a large suitcase from Woolworth – he recalled later that he thought it was ideal because it, 'had a zipper with a leather buckle going around the suitcase.'

Having crammed Tuomi's body into the suitcase, Dahmer took a taxi back to his grandmother's house and his own apartment in the basement. The driver, although he complained about the weight, helped him drag the heavy item indoors. One week later Jeff dismembered the corpse, filleted the bones from the body before cutting the flesh into pieces small enough to handle, then placed the flesh into plastic bags. He wrapped the bones inside a sheet and pounded them with a sledgehammer. The entire butchery process took about two hours to complete then he disposed of Tuomi's remains – excluding the head – in the trash.

For the next fortnight, Dahmer retained Steve's head wrapped in a blanket, then he boiled the head down in a mixture of bleach and Soilex (an alkali-based industrial detergent) in an effort to preserve the skull, which he then used as a stimulus for masturbation. Eventually, the skull was rendered too brittle by this bleaching process, so Dahmer pulverised it and threw it away.

Clearly this second kill was a waypoint in Jeff Dahmer's life. He had got away with murdering Steven Hicks. I believe that even if he had been arrested that night by the police who came across him driving, he could have put forward some extenuating circumstances – the stress of his parents' acrimonious divorce for one. He could have even argued that he and Steven had got into a drunken fight and Hicks had accidentally hit his head and died. I am sure that even a halfwit public defender blowing clouds of mitigation into the jury's yard could have got Jeff off the hook on this one. But the murder of Tuomi was something quite different.

This was a deliberate act, whether Dahmer was sober or not. Since Tuomi had gone to the hotel room specifically for sex, there could be no reason whatsoever to kill him – unless Dahmer's needs involved more than an act of mutual sexual intercourse. Dahmer would later lie, telling police that he'd had no intention of killing Stephen Tuomi – trawling out more-or-less the same lame duck excuse as he did in trying to later mitigate the Hicks homicide. 'I passed out,' he said, 'and when I came to I was laying on top of Tuomi, and he was dead. I realised that I'd killed him and needed to get rid of the body, so I went out and bought a suitcase,' adding, 'which suited my purpose exactly.'

As the result of Tuomi's murder Dahmer must have acknowledged that homicide and dismemberment were now absolutely necessary to satisfy his uncontrollable and deviant sexual fantasies. The fifteen murders that followed leave no possible doubt of that. He had perhaps tried to fight these impulses before. He admitted much later that, just before he was banned from the bathhouses, he recalls trying to resist the temptation to hurt someone by looking in the newspaper obituary column and finding a death notice for any nineteen or twenty-year-old male. He even attended a funeral. When he viewed the corpse in the casket, he knew it was the perfect body. After the burial he went to the graveyard and tried to dig the body up. He told police he failed because the ground was too hard and that whilst trying to dig he was attacked by the graveyard's dog.

Stephen Tuomi is memorialised at the Holy Family Catholic Cemetery, Ontonagon, Michigan. But his remains were never found despite police searches after Dahmer's arrest. As a result, Dahmer was never charged with the murder of Steven Tuomi – even after he had confessed to the crime.

James 'Jamie' Edward Doxator

While researching my subjects, dipping quill into ink and scribbling away, I always try to remain bipartisan, and to carefully consider the advice, views and opinions of others who know what they are talking about when often I don't. Yes, I take stock of what they say in sterling efforts to provide my readers with a balanced appraisal of any issue in question. This book is no exception – that was until I had the misfortune of bumping into a well-meaning member of The Salvation Army who seemed to know a thing or two about Jeffrey Dahmer.

'You know, Christopher, last week my husband and I read about Jeff in a magazine while we were in our doctor's waiting room,' she said above the sound of her band playing *Nearer, My God, to Thee* in a high wind. Rattling her tin, she suggested that 'the long periods of Jeff's isolation and feelings of being rejected and self-imposed loneliness were his heartfelt desperate efforts to find himself.' Looking at me with the sort of imploring watery eyes that only a determined tin-rattler can, she added: 'Wilfred and I are visiting one of our daughters in

El Paso next year, maybe we will drive up to visit Jeff and pray with him.'

'But that's 1,500 miles from your daughter's place. And you can't visit with him anyway,' I said.

'Why not?' she asked.

'Because he's dead, *that*'s *why not*. He was murdered in prison twenty-seven years ago.'

For a moment she remained silent, then said, 'Well, it must have been an old magazine, then.'

If I'd had some loose change I would have gladly dropped it in her tin – alas I did not!

On 16 January 1988, Dahmer got talking to a fourteen-year-old Native-American boy called James Doxator at a bus stop outside Club 219. He asked James if he would like to earn $50 posing for nude photos. Dahmer and Doxator went back to West Allis on a bus. They had sex in his basement room in his grandmother's house. Then Dahmer gave the lad a drink heavily laced with a sleeping potion. When Jamie fell unconscious, Jeff strangled him on the floor of the cellar. He left the corpse for a week before dismembering it in much the same manner as he'd done with Tuomi. Apparently, Grandma Catherine rarely visited the cellar and it's a jolly good thing she didn't too, bless her. Jeff then placed all of Jamie's remains – excluding the head – in the garbage. Again, he boiled the skull, rendering the flesh down, and initially retained it before pulverising it with the sledgehammer.

Much later, after Dahmer's arrest, the police interrogator looked up from his notebook to ask if there was anything distinctive about James Doxator by which he might be identified. Dahmer recalled quite vividly that he had two scars near his nipples. Jamie was living at 1010 West

Pierce Street, Milwaukee, at the time of his death. Like Stephen, his remains have never been found although he is memorialised in the Stockbridge Indian Burial Grounds, Bowler, Shawano County, Wisconsin. His mother, Debbie Vega, speaking in 1991 after the arrest of her son's murderer said: 'I just want to forget about it for a little while. Jamie ran away from our Milwaukee home three years ago after fighting with his stepfather.'

Grandma Catherine was now finally cottoning on that something was going on in her home. She complained to Lionel and Shari about a bad smell emanating from her garage. If it had been the garbage, surely the sweet stench would have gone away after the trash had been collected – but it lingered on. Lionel was quick to come over and investigate and noted that there was an odoriferous residue on the floor – something black and slimy. However, despite the unmistakable stench of decomposing flesh, Lionel Dahmer bought Jeffrey's bullshit hook, line and sinker.

Richard Guerrero

'Richard GUERRERO, H/M, DOB: 12/12/65, of 3332 N. 1ˢᵗ St. Reported missing to the Milwaukee PD on 3/29/88. He was identified by the suspect as being a victim in these series of homicides. This homicide occurred in the City of West Allis at the home of the suspect's (Dahmer) grandmother and there are no remains.'

FBI file

Two months elapsed before Jeffrey Dahmer killed again. On 24 March 1988, in The Phoenix, a bar at 789 N. Jefferson Street, not far from Club 219, he met twenty-three-year-old, bisexual Richard Guerrero. The Phoenix was at the southern anchor of an area of several gay bars in a one block area. Richard was last seen leaving his family's North Side home apparently to visit a friend in Milwaukee. He had only $3 in his pocket and no wallet or other identification. The youngest of six siblings, Guerrero was around five-foot six-inches tall and weighed 130 pounds. He had brown hair and brown eyes. Dahmer was attracted by the graceful, slightly built man so he offered him $50 to come back to his grandmother's home and spend the rest of the night with him. Here they had oral sex and Dahmer offered Guerrero a drink laced with crushed sleeping pills. When the lad was unconscious Dahmer strangled him with a leather strap. He then performed oral sex on the corpse then dismembered him in the garage, placing the bloody remains in the garbage.

The lad was devoted to his family and, when he disappeared, Guerrero's frantic parents hired a private detective and circulated leaflets with their son's description. They even hired a psychic to try and find their son. But they were still searching three years later when Dahmer confessed to his murder.

Dahmer's next victim, Ronald Flowers, had a narrow escape. On 23 April, Grandma Catherine became suspicious when she heard two voices coming from her grandson's basement room. He had lured another lad back and was giving the lad a drugged coffee when both heard Catherine call out, 'Is that you, Jeff?' Dahmer replied, indicating that he was alone, but she suspected otherwise. Because of this interruption, Dahmer decided not to kill, instead he waited until Flowers became unconscious before taking him to the hospital.

Nonetheless, Catherine was now sick and tired of Jeff's habit of bringing young men back to her house late at night and becoming even more concerned about the awful smells coming from both the basement room and her garage. In September 1988, she finally decided that she would no longer tolerate the smells and Jeff's drunkenness. Jeff moved into an apartment on North 25th Street, Milwaukee for more 'Corpse Love'.

Corpse Love

'He was the closest thing I ever saw to Sherlock Holmes. With his precision and his dedication there was nobody better at that type of work.'

Former LAPD homicide detective on Detective Pierce Brooks

By the time he left his grandmother's home, Dahmer had established a working modus operandi. Like so many serial sex killers, this MO would become polished and refined through practice and premeditation. Luring people back to their kill places in an 'organised way' is not an MO unique to Dahmer. It is also common that serial predators will know where to hunt for their victims. British serial killer Peter Sutcliffe trawled the red-light districts of Leeds and Bradford looking for sex workers and lone women. Dahmer, likewise, knew where to find his victims – young, predominantly gay men. In terms of victim selection, Dahmer can be seen as an 'opportunist killer' in that he seemed to select victims at random. But Jeffrey Dahmer knew precisely *where* to hunt for them.

He had figured out ways to persuade them to come home with him where he could isolate them. He had methods of rendering his prey unconscious and of killing them. And he had figured out a method for disposing of his victims' bodies, thereafter. He had not yet been caught. His motive was sexual gratification. Dahmer was a necrophile.

The etymology of the word 'necrophilia' comes from the Greek 'nekros' (death) and 'philia' (love or affection). There is some evidence that members of the Moche civilization, in what is now Peru, believed that sex with dead bodies provided a spiritual connection with the deceased – each to their own, I suppose! For our purposes however, necrophilia is now taken to mean a sexual attraction to dead bodies, and it is a specified paraphiliac disorder involving recurrent and intense sexual interest in corpses.

Wayne Petherick and Natasha Petherick write in *Homicide* (2019), 'Although the media may give the illusion of a more common prevalence of violent and unusual crimes, necrophilia is even rarer than sexual homicide. The true prevalence of necrophilia is unknown given that this paraphilia is most often carried out in secret, with the victim unable to report the act.' What a blindingly obvious last statement that is, too.

Necrophilia was first documented in Richard Freiherr von Krafft-Ebing's *Psychopathia Sexualis* (1886). Since then there has been a lot of variation discovered in those who engage in this behaviour and subsequently many attempts to produce a cohesive classification. There are those who receive pleasure (not necessarily sexual) from being near the dead – for example during the mummification or preservation of a deceased loved one. Then there are those that are aroused by touching the dead. And finally there are those who exclusively require sex with the dead.

Aside from mortuary attendants and funeral home workers who have been known to have been caught sexually abusing corpses, there are individuals who have dug up graves in order to obtain a dead body to have sex with. More commonly there are serial murderers such as Ed Kemper, Ed Gein, Dennis Nilsen, Peter Kürten, and Gary Ridgway who have abused – sexually and grotesquely – their deceased victims.

Anil Aggrawal, in *Encyclopedia of Forensic and Legal Medicine* (Second Edition), 2016,[16] refers to necrophilia – also known as necrophilism, necrolagnia, necrocoitus, necroclesis, and thanatophilia – saying '…may also be seen by itself or in association with a number of other paraphilias, namely: sadism; cannibalism; vampirism (the drinking of blood from a person or animal); necrophagia (eating the flesh of the dead); necropedophilia (sexual attraction to the corpses of children), and necrozoophilia (sexual attraction to the corpses of, or killing of animals – also known as necrobestiality).'

Phew, that was a big verbally intrusive mouthful wasn't it? Did I previously advise you that this is most certainly *not* a pre-meal subject? If I didn't, I damn well *should have* done. Because, hey, guys and gals, we haven't even started yet!

Very often the corpses used for sexual purposes are not farm fresh, but rather exhumed in a putrefied or mummified condition – some people have got no class at all have they? Others prefer just the bones. Necrophagists actually feed on decaying bodies to get sexual pleasure and these warped individuals are different from cannibals, who prefer fresh meat, or who consume dead loved ones for spiritual purposes. 'Enough, enough already, Christopher,' I hear you moan, but as we are dealing with Jeff Dahmer in this book, I am compelled to go on. You see there is a vast spectrum of necrophagists – from those who merely want to lick the genitals or breasts of a dead person, to people who just want to devour specific parts.

Jeffrey Dahmer's sexual fantasies involved the dead. He had been ready to dig up a corpse in order to satisfy them. He selected, trawled, entrapped his victims. He had sex with some of them while they were alive, as he murdered them and also post-mortem.

Keison Sinthasomphone

Having now been thrown out of his grandmother's home, there can be no doubt that Jeff Dahmer intended to use his freedom to give full rein to his morbid sexual urges. Within twenty-four hours of moving into a one-bedroomed place at 808 N.25th Street, he was in trouble with the police. On 26 September 1988 he met a thirteen-year-old Laotian boy named Keison Sinthasomphone and lured him back to his apartment on the promise of paying him $50 for taking nude photographs. At his apartment, Dahmer served the kid Irish Cream spiked with sleeping pills. When Dahmer unzipped Keison's pants and tried to grab his penis, the boy fled.

The teenager managed to get home, after which his father noticed that something was not quite right with his son. Keison seemed to be having trouble walking and speaking, so Mr Sinthasomphone took him to a hospital. Tests revealed the presence of drugs in the boy's system.

Jeffrey Dahmer was arrested that night at the Ambrosia Chocolate Factory. He claimed that he didn't know that young Sinthasomphone was a minor. He was charged with sexual assault and enticing a child for immoral purposes. He spent a week in prison then was released on bail to live once again with his grandmother.

Anthony Lee Sears

'I don't know why I'm so evil. I don't have any definite answers myself. It's a process that doesn't happen overnight. When you depersonalise a person as an object, an object for pleasure, not a living, breathing, human being.

Hunting itself was a thrill; never knowing who I'd meet… nice-looking maybe… how much fun we'd have.

The killing was a means to an end.'

Jeffrey Dahmer

Twenty-six-year-old Anthony Lee Sears was a friendly, good-looking, African/American and wanted to become a male model. Anthony was a bisexual and, in 1989, he had a girlfriend and had just been appointed manager of a popular, pie-focused Bakers Square Restaurant on Elm Grove, Milwaukee.

On 25 March, Jeff with a friend called Bob Keel, went drinking in the La Cage on 2nd Street, where they overheard two young men, Sears and his friend, Jeffrey Connor. They were talking about modelling, so Dahmer engaged them in conversation. At closing time, and on the promise of being paid to have nude photographs taken, Sears made the fateful decision to accompany Dahmer back to his grandmother's place. Dahmer seemed to have been worried that, as he was still on bail, the police might be watching his apartment at 808 N.25th Street. Connor then drove Sears, Keel and Dahmer to West Allis. Before Connor let Spears go, he reminded him that he was going to spend time with his family over Easter and asked him to call him in case he needed a ride home.

Once inside his grandmother's home, Dahmer offered his guest a Micky Finn and they had oral sex. The grim routine was then repeated almost without variation. Sears was drugged then strangled and his body was violated by Dahmer. The following morning, his corpse was placed in the bathtub where Dahmer decapitated it, before attempting to flay it. He stripped off the flesh and pulverised the bones, which were thrown into the trash.

According to Sears's mother, Marilyn, her son was planning to meet her the following day to celebrate his recent promotion. 'But he never showed up,' she said, tearfully, to police. While searching for her son in West Allis, Marilyn had had an eerie feeling when she arrived outside Catherine Dahmer's house and asked the police to check the place out. They refused, despite the fact that the neighbours had noticed a sweet stench emanating from the garage for several weeks.

In his statements to police after his arrest in 1991, Dahmer said that he found Sears 'exceptionally attractive.' Anthony was the first victim from whom he permanently retained any body parts aside from the skull. He preserved both Sears's head and genitals in acetone as 'mementos'.

A year later, when he moved into the Oxford Apartments, 924 North 25th Street, Apartment 213, he would take Sears's mummified head – which he painted to look a fake head – and genitals with him.

Anthony Sears's remains are buried in the Arlington Park Cemetery, Greenfield, Milwaukee County.

Raymond Lamont Smith

'He (the defendant) gave the man a drink which was drugged and the man fell asleep; that he (the defendant) then strangled the man and removed the man's clothing and had oral sex with him; further, that he dismembered the body but kept the skull and later painted it; further that he (the defendant) identified photographs of Raymond Lamont SMITH as being photographs of the man to whom he had done this.'

Official police document

On 23 May 1989, Dahmer came before the court for sentencing for second degree aggravated sexual assault and of enticing a child for immoral purposes. Assistant District Attorney, Gale G. Shelton, had recognised instinctively that any man who would drug a teenage boy like Keison Sinthasomphone for sex was highly dangerous and needed to be kept out of society for a long time. She fiercely argued for a prison sentence of five years describing Dahmer as 'evasive, manipulative and unrepentant.' In her statement to the court she said:

> 'In my judgement it is absolutely crystal clear that the prognosis for treatment for Mr Dahmer in the community is extremely bleak. His perception of what he did wrong was choosing too young a victim; and that's all he did wrong is a part of the problem. He appears to be cooperative and perceptive but anything that goes below the surface indicates that the deep-seated anger and deep-seated psychological problems that he is unwilling to deal with.'

Dahmer's attorney, Gerald Boyle, countered that the assault on the Laotian boy was 'a one-off offence and would never happen again.' He argued, on behalf of his client:

> 'Jeffrey needs treatment, not prison. We don't have multiple offenses here. I believe he was caught at the point where it could have got worse, which means it's a blessing in disguise.'

Boyle must have thought differently when his client soon turned out to be one of the most heinous serial killers in U.S. criminal history! Boyle later fell from grace for violating the rules of conduct in two 2015 criminal cases in Kenosha and Brown counties and for accepting bribes.

Dahmer revealed considerable skill as an actor during the hearing by representing himself as contrite and ashamed. He pleaded:

'I am an alcoholic and a homosexual with sexual problems. What I've done is very serious. I've never been in this position, nothing this awful before. This is a nightmare come true to me. If anything would shock me out of my past behaviour patterns it's this. The one thing I have on my mind that is stable, and gives me some source of pride, is my job.'

Presiding over the courtroom was Judge William Gardner. Thought of as being 'too priestly' by many of his colleagues Gardner was touched by Dahmer's appeal. A former member of the Wisconsin Bar Association and a Milwaukee County District Attorney, Gardner regarded this clean-cut boy as obviously needing psychiatric help. Lionel did too and wrote to the judge begging him to get Jeffrey some help.

Uncomfortably caught between two legal hard rocks the judge let Dahmer off lightly; five years on probation and a year on a work release programme where he could continue to do his job at the chocolate factory during the day. Dahmer was also required to register as a sex offender and undergo more psychological testing with Dr Krembs, who assessed Dahmer as having a: '...very boring and lifeless existence with no social outlets, such as friends or hobbies.' The doctor reported that Dahmer's life was: '...monomaniacally directed which is an excellent breeding ground for depression,' then concluded that a 'major relapse was just a matter of time.'

Born on 10 August 1957, Raymond Lamont Smith was last seen alive on 29 May 1989. Dahmer met him at a Club 219 and offered him $50.00 to pose for sex photos. Smith, a slender man with a slight moustache, had been in and out of trouble all his life. He had been incarcerated for burglary and was at the time making money as a sex worker. He had a daughter in Rockford, Illinois. Back at his place Dahmer drugged him with a sleeping pill-laced drink and strangled him to death. Dahmer said that the following day he went out and bought a Polaroid camera which he used to take many photos of Smith's corpse in sexually suggestive positions. Dahmer dismembered the body in the bathroom. He boiled the legs, arms, and pelvis in a steel kettle with Soilex, allowing him to then rinse the bones in a sink. He dissolved the remainder of the skeleton – excluding the skull – in a container filled with acid. He later spray-painted Smith's skull, which he placed alongside the skull of Sears upon a black towel inside a metal filing cabinet. At the time of Smith's disappearance no one had reported Sears missing to any police agency. He was identified through dental records. His grandmother was notified of his death at 10 a.m. on 25 July 1991. Dahmer would later say at his trial that as he removed Raymond's shirt before the dismembering started, he discovered a tattoo on his chest. It consisted of the name 'Cash D', with pitchforks going out of the letter points on the word 'Cash'.

There appears to be a discrepancy in other references over a claim made by Dahmer that he invited another young man who has never been identified back to his apartment on, or about, 27 May. On this occasion, Dahmer had accidentally taken the drink laden with sedatives intended for consumption by his guest. When he awoke the following day, he discovered that the intended victim had stolen several items of his clothing, cash and a watch. Dahmer told his probation officer that he had been robbed but didn't report this theft to the police.

Edward 'Eddie' Warren Smith

'I felt rotten about Smith's murder. I was unable to keep any of the body parts.'

Jeffrey Dahmer

Happy-go-lucky Eddie Smith was born on 2 August 1962 and lived at 3606 W. 11th Street, Milwaukee with his sister, Caroline. The house was very similar to Grandma's place in West Allis. The Smith family consisted of eight brothers and four sisters, and it was common knowledge that Eddie was gay. He wore heavy make-up and was open about his sexuality. At six-foot three and 165 pounds, one *might* have thought they he could have taken care of himself. On the night of 14 June he told Caroline that he was going into the city for a night out in the clubs. He wouldn't be late home because the next day he had every intention of attending Milwaukee's Gay Pride parade. Eddie didn't come home and was eventually reported missing on 23 June 1990.

Dahmer had met up with him and persuaded him to come back to his apartment. There he drugged him and then strangled him. On this occasion rather than immediately acidifying the skeleton or repeating previous processes of bleaching, he placed Smith's skeleton in his freezer for several months in the hope that it would not retain moisture. Unfortunately for Dahmer, this process didn't work, therefore, the skeleton would have to be 'acidified'. Dahmer accidentally destroyed the skull when he placed it into his oven to dry – a process that caused the skull to explode.

In a sick twist, the following April, Caroline answered her telephone.

'Don't bother looking for your brother,' said the soft voice.

'Why not?'

'Because he's dead,' came the ice-cold answer.

'How do you know that?'

'Because I killed him,' said Dahmer, as he had boasted with other victims' families before. Edward's family was notified of Edward's death at 9.30 p.m. on 29 July 1991.

Ernest Marquez Miller

'It was my way of remembering their appearance, their physical beauty. I always wanted to keep...if I couldn't keep them with me whole, I at least could keep their skeletons.'

Dahmer, *The Journal Times*, 8 February 1993

Born on 5 May 1967, Ernest Marquez-Miller was a handsome black dancer who was visiting from Chicago where he intended to start training at a dance school that autumn. He was last seen alive after leaving a friend's home on 3 September 1990 and was reported as missing to the police by relatives the following day.

After his arrest, Dahmer told homicide detectives that he had encountered the young man outside an adult bookstore on the corner of North 27th Street. Miller had agreed to go with him back to his apartment to allow him to listen to his heart and stomach for $50.00. One rather thinks that if some strange young man approached you on the street with such a bizarre request, one might politely decline the most generous offer, and leave him with a mouthful of broken teeth. But not Ernest – far from it! When Dahmer tried to instigate oral sex Ernest told his host 'That'll cost you extra.' Jeffrey gave Ernest a drink. On this occasion, however, Dahmer was only in possession of two sleeping pills so as Ernest started to lose consciousness, to expedite the kill, he slashed the youth's throat with the same knife he used for dismembering. Ernest Miller bled out in minutes. After taking photos of Ernest's body with his Polaroid camera, he dismembered the corpse in the bathtub. He wrapped the heart, biceps and portions of flesh from the legs in plastic bags and placed them in his refrigerator to cook and eat later. He boiled the remaining flesh and organs into a 'jelly-like substance' using Soilex. Again, this allowed him to rinse the flesh off of the skeleton – which he intended to retain but needed preserving first of all. He placed the bones into a bleach solution for 24 hours before allowing them to dry upon a cloth for a week. The severed head was initially placed in the fridge before also being stripped of flesh. Dahmer then painted and coated the skull with enamel. Miller was later identified through dental records. His parents were notified of his death at 8.30 a.m. on 26 July 1991.

David Courtney Thomas

African/American, David Thomas was born on 21 December 1967. In September 1990, he was living at 6432 W. Birch Street, Milwaukee although he had no real permanent residence. He'd lived on and off with a girlfriend for years and had a three-year-old daughter whom he visited regularly. Thomas's parents hadn't heard from him for a month, and he was on probation for retail theft

Three weeks after the Miller murder, on 24 September 1990, Dahmer met Thomas at the Grand Avenue Mall, 275 W. Wisconsin Avenue. Using his usual chat-up line he persuaded the twenty-two-year-old to return to his apartment for a few drinks, with a bonus of money if he would pose for photographs. David must have found the cash offer appealing because he accepted. Jeffrey gave him the usual drugged drink but then decided that Thomas was not his type at all and that he had no desire for sex. But since Thomas was now drugged and might be angry when he woke up, he was killed anyway. Dahmer kept no trophies from this murder, but he did take photographs of the dismemberment process and David's severed head. It was these photographs which confirmed his identity when shown to his sister after Dahmer's arrest.

Following this homicide, Dahmer didn't commit murder for almost five months, although he later told police that on at least five occasions between October 1990 and February 1991, he unsuccessfully attempted to lure men to his apartment. At around this time, he is also known to have complained to his probation officer of constant feelings of both anxiety and depression, with frequent references to his sexuality, his solitary lifestyle, and financial difficulties.

Curtis Durrell Straughter

'It's not sparing me by not letting me know of the specifics of Curtis's death.'

Dorothy Straughter, mother of the victim

Dahmer's first murder of 1991 was that of a seventeen-year-old black homosexual named Curtis Straughter, whose ambition was to become a model. Born on 16 April 1973, Curtis lived at 3628 N. 19th Street, Milwaukee. He was last seen on 18 February 1991 when Dahmer saw him standing at a bus stop in freezing, rainy weather and enticed him to his apartment with the usual offer of money for nude photographs and sex. While they were engaging in oral sex in the now evil-smelling apartment, Straughter began to flag as the sleeping potion took effect. After his final arrest, Dahmer told police, 'I had Straughter on my bed, he was drugged and started to pass out. Then he rolled off the bed and knocked over a black table which had two griffins on it each named 'Leon' and 'Apal'... These were part of my occult stuff, and symbolised personal power and made it that I did not have to answer to anyone.' Dahmer then took a leather strap and strangled Straughter. He then dissected the body and recorded the process with his camera. Once again, he kept the skull.

All that remained of Curtis Straughter was his skull and it is buried at the Holy Cross Cemetery and Mausoleum, Milwaukee.

Errol Scott Lindsey

The murder of nineteen-year-old Errol Lindsey on 7 April 1991 begins with a quality of déjà vu. Born on 3 March 1972, Lindsey lived at 1119 N. 24th Place, Milwaukee. He was a member of the choir at the Greater Spring Hill Missionary Baptist Church; he was a guy everybody took a liking to as soon as they met him, with author Don Davis describing Errol as having a 'wide smile breaking through hostile barriers.'

On that day, Errol had been shopping at The Grand Avenue Mall, 275 W Wisconsin Avenue, and had returned to his mother's flat on 24th Street. He then went out again to get a key cut, and it was then that he met Dahmer. Lindsey was not gay, but he agreed to go home with Dahmer when he was offered money for nude photographs.

Back at Dahmer's place, Lindsey was drugged. Dahmer then drilled a hole into his skull and poured in hydrochloric acid. According to Dahmer, the aim was to induce a Zombie-like unresistant, submissive state in the young man. Lindsey awoke after this experiment complaining of a headache and asking for the time. Dahmer strangled

Errol then had oral sex with the body. Dahmer decapitated the lad and retained his skull then flayed the body, placing the skin in a solution of cold water and salt for several weeks in the hope of permanently keeping it. It was with reluctance that he later disposed of Linsey's skin when he noted that it had become frayed and brittle

Errol was reported missing by his sister Rita Isbell on 11 April. His mother was notified of his death on 26 July. Rita was visibly emotional at the trial of her brother's murderer. She shouted, 'Jeffrey, I hate you. You are Satan you Motherfucker. Never again Jeffrey! Never!' and charged at the table where he was sitting with his lawyers.

Anthony 'Tony' Hughes

Thirty-one-year-old Tony Hughes was a deaf mute who loved to dance. Tony was born on 26 August 1959, and lived at 211 S. Carol Street, Madison. He was reported as missing to the Madison PD on 31 May 1991, and was last seen by a friend at Club 219 on 24th September 1991. Dahmer accosted him outside the club that night, and because of Tony's limitations he made his proposition in writing: '$50 for some photographs'.

Back at Dahmer's apartment, Hughes was offered the sleeping potion, then he was strangled and dismembered. Dahmer had become so casual in the act of murder that he simply left the body lying in the bedroom for a day or so before beginning the dismemberment process. That was, after all, no riskier than having an apartment with skulls and body parts in almost plain view.

Tony's skull and vertebrae were found in Dahmer's apartment upon his arrest. His mother was notified of his death at 2.50 p.m. on 5 July 1991. He had no criminal antecedents.

Stinking to High Heaven

'An oppressive odor of decay now mingled with the stench of mold and seemed to clutch at the very breath in their lungs.'

Kaoru Kurimato (1953-2009), *The Leopard Mask*

Decomposing human bodies emit a distinct chemical cocktail that separates them from other decaying animals. Human corpses emit a unique five-chemical cocktail – comprised of 3-methylbutyl pentanoate, 3-methylbutyl-methylbutyrate, 3-methylbutyl 2-methylbutrate, butyl pentanoate and propyl hexanoate – all these combined creates something quite unique on planet earth. Well, I betcha didn't know that did you? These five chemicals are part of a group of molecules called esters. Esters are produced by degrading muscles, carbohydrates and fat tissues which are responsible for the strong, sharp smells emitted by fruits like pineapples and raspberries – in a nutshell the human smell of death is a bit 'fruity'. The mixture of these compounds can be used to train cadaver dogs. And by now, Dahmer's neighbours were getting some experience of this unique scent too.

By 1991, residents of the Oxford Apartments had repeatedly complained to the building's manager, Sopa Princewill, of the foul odours emanating from apartment 213, as well as the sounds of falling objects and the occasional buzz of a chainsaw. On several occasions Princewill did contact Jeffrey in response to these complaints. Dahmer initially excused the putrid smells as being caused by his freezer breaking down and causing the contents to be 'spoiled'. On later occasions, he informed Princewill that the continuing wafting stench was down to several of his tropical fish that had recently died. He assured the manager that he would take care of the matter. So if your Zebra Danios or your Popeyed Guppy gets fin rot and floats upside down to the surface, flush it down the loo or the smell will have the local council on your back in a heartbeat. Dahmer had gotten used to the stench – he had become 'nose blind'. If you really want to know what it was like to live next door to Dahmer, Princewill later wrote a book titled *The Prime Target: Life alongside serial killer Jeffrey Dahmer inside the Oxford Apartments*.

Konerak Sinthasomphone

Dahmer's next murder was, frankly, an unholy clusterfuck. Victim number thirteen was a fourteen-year-old Laotian boy named Konerak Sinthasomphone. In a bizarre and tragic twist of fate it turned out that Konerak was the brother of Keison, who had escaped Dahmer's clutches back in 1988 although Dahmer was not aware of this at the time. On the afternoon of 26 May 1991, Dahmer spotted Konerak on Wisconsin Avenue, a short distance from his apartment. Using his usual chat-up line, Dahmer lured the lad back to his apartment with an offer of money if he posed for Polaroid photos. Konerak reluctantly agreed. After two pictures had been taken of the young teen in his underwear, Dahmer drugged him into unconsciousness and performed oral sex on him.

There seems to be some confusion as to what actually happened after Konerak was drugged. Some say that Dahmer drilled a single hole in the boy's skull and injected hydrochloric acid into the frontal lobe in an attempt to turn him into a zombie. Thinking that his victim would remain unconscious, Dahmer went out to a bar for a drink and to buy a pack of beer. However, Konerak woke up almost as soon as Dahmer left the stinking apartment and he saw the decomposing body of Tony Hughes in the bedroom. Terrified, working purely on instinct, he ran naked down the concrete stairs and into the street crying for help. Stumbling along in the darkness, Konerak was spotted by two local cousins, Sandra Smith and Nicole Childress. He had red patches of blood on his behind and was almost incoherent when, almost immediately, a tall white male with a wispy moustache appeared and made a grab for the boy as he was being held by Sandra.

Sandra and Nicole were streetwise girls so Sandra would not turn the kid loose. She held onto his arm while they went to a nearby payphone to dial 911 – she wanted the emergency services there immediately. 'I'm on 25th and State, and there is this young man. He's buck-naked. He has been beaten up… He is really hurt… He needs some help,' she told the emergency dispatcher.

First on scene with its flashing light bar was fire engine '32' followed by two blue-and-white squad cars from the Milwaukee PD. What followed would blacken the name of the police department for decades to follow. Capt. John A. Balcerzak (thirty-six), Officer Joseph 'Joe' T. Gabrish (twenty-three), Officer Richard Porubcan (twenty-five) and an unidentified MPD trainee were the officers attending the scene. They seemed totally unconcerned when they found a naked and bleeding young man, and another man arguing with the girls. In a later pathetic effort to excuse their utter incompetence, the cops said they thought that the blood on Konerak's behind had come from a scraped knee. The officers split them up and waved the fire engine containing medics away after one of them wrapped a blanket around the dazed lad to cover his nakedness. By now a crowd had gathered. Dahmer insisted that Konerak was his boyfriend and was drunk after a lovers' tiff. The police wanted to get matters under control as soon as possible so they decided to go back to Dahmer's apartment. The girls persisted because they knew something was wrong. They insisted that the cops take down their names as witnesses but were told to 'butt out'.

Eventually the girls rushed back to Sandra's mother Glenda Cleveland who lived close to the Oxford Apartments and angrily blurted out what had happened. A white man possibly molesting a young man of colour rang alarm bells, so a now infuriated Glenda telephoned the police – a call that would eventually be broadcast around the world. The police dispatcher told her that everything had been taken care of. The young lad was an adult and he's now back with his boyfriend in his boyfriend's apartment. 'Ma'am, I can't be any clearer than this,' the cop told her, 'it's as positive as I can be. I can't do anything about someone's sexual preferences in life.' A couple of days later, Glenda called back after she had read a newspaper article about the disappearance of a Laotian boy named Konerak Sinthasomphone. He looked exactly like the lad her daughter and niece had seen trying to escape from Dahmer. The police never sent anyone to talk to her. Glenda even contacted the Milwaukee field office of the FBI, but nothing came of that either.

Meanwhile, in apartment 213, Dahmer seemed apologetic. Although it smelt bad, the place was neat and tidy and Konerak's clothes were folded neatly on the sofa alongside some Polaroid photos of Konerak in black bikini briefs. Speaking calmly, not in any way nervous, the well-spoken and intelligent Dahmer said that he was ashamed that his lover had caused such a ruckus and promised that this would never happen again. He didn't smell of booze while the young Lao seemed drunk and was incoherent. Dahmer falsely explained that his boyfriend had been drinking and had run out onto the street. He had been trying to bring him home when the two girls got involved. It had happened before. They were lovers and often argued. The cops looked at the befuddled Konerak propped up on the sofa, then back to Dahmer. 'How old is that lad?' asked an officer. Dahmer lied. 'Nineteen,' he said glibly. 'He looks very young for his age, doesn't he?'

The officers now felt that this was becoming a waste of their valuable time when the city was rife with drug dealers, fights, stabbings, shootings, muggers and thieves. This was just another squabble between two gays. They could see the Polaroid photos of Konerak in his underwear. So what? That backed up Dahmer's story. Did they ignore all of the photos of other boys and young men taped to the walls? If they'd looked, they'd have uncovered photos of several dismembered bodies. What about the godforsaken stench that permeated the place? Balcerzak later claiming he noted a strange scent of excrement inside the apartment. The odour was coming from the rotting body of Hughes which lay inside the bedroom at that very moment. One cop peeked his head around the bedroom door but didn't really take a good look and missed the body entirely. Had they taken the time to carry out out a radio check, they would have realised they were standing right next to a violent sex offender. *But they didn't.* Had this been done they would have learned of Dahmer's conviction in 1989 of second-degree sexual assault on a teenage boy called Keison Sinthasomphone. They would have learned that Mr Dahmer was still on probation for that crime. If they had insisted on confirming the boy's identity rather than believing Dahmer, they would have learned not only that Konerak was Keison's brother but that he was just fourteen.

If only the police had asked a few more questions, checked a few more facts... *if* only. Instead, they simply left... They left Konerak alone with a flesh-eating monster – the Milwaukee Cannibal. Any chance of saving his life went with the shiny badges as they walked out of the door. They missed the chance to stop one of the most infamous serial killers the world has ever known.

When one cop called in to the precinct to report the incident – 'Intoxicated Asian, naked male, was returned to his boyfriend' – laughter could be heard in the background. 'My partner is going to get deloused at the station.'

Later, when this failure of policing came to light it caused a worldwide storm, much in the same way as the murder of forty-six-year-old black American, George Floyd, in Minneapolis, on 25 May 2020. Captain Balcerzak was fired for having handed over the injured child to Dahmer, despite bystanders' protests. He appealed his termination and was subsequently reinstated. In May 2005, he was elected president of the Milwaukee Police Association. He vacated his position as president on 31 December 2009. He retired from the Milwaukee PD in 2017. Officer

Porubcan was also sacked. Gabrish was dismissed after having enjoyed a very hard-working career, rising through the ranks over eleven years to become captain. He had earned his Bachelors and Masters of Science degrees in Criminal Justice, whilst attending Northwestern University School of Police Staff and Command. He was named Police Officer of the Year in 2011 by both the Grafton and Ozaukee County American Legion. In 2019 he received the FBI Milwaukee 'Citizens Academy Unsung Hero Award'. He retired on 10 October 2019.

As for Konerak, what happened to him is almost too unbearable to think about. Upon the departure of the cops from his apartment, the now infuriated Dahmer bored another hole using his electric 'Sear's Craftsman's' drill into the unconscious boy's skull and, using a hypodermic needle, administered another injection of acid which proved agonisingly fatal. The following day, 28 May, Dahmer took a day's leave from work to devote himself to the dismemberment of the bodies of Konerak and Tony Hughes using a saw blade, a white-handled knife, an ECO knife with a one-inch blade, and a three-inch Sheffield knife.

Dahmer retained both skulls. All that was left of Konerak after Dahmer's arrest was his skull, some of his vertebrae and some of his teeth. The Sinthasomphones launched a legal action against the City of Milwaukee on March 5, 1992.

Matt Cleveland Turner

Born on 3 July 1970, in Chicago, Illinois, Turner was never reported as a 'misper' (missing person) to police. Dahmer's account of this homicide came after his arrest. He recalled that on 30 June 1991 he travelled to Chicago to attend the Gay Pride parade and met twenty-year-old Turner at the Greyhound bus station at 630 W. Harrison Street. Matt had been living in a halfway house for runaway teens at the time, and the young black man was flattered by the tall, white man's attention. After a short conversation Matt accepted an offer to return to Milwaukee with Jeffrey where he would be paid for a 'professional' photo shoot. Returning together from Chicago on a bus they used a City Vet cab to take them from 433 W, St, Paul Avenue to 25th Street and Dahmer's home. Here, Dahmer drugged Turner who almost instantly passed out. Dahmer then strangled him with a leather strap and dismembered the body. His head and internal organs were placed in separate bags in the freezer.

Initially identification of Matt Turner was made from severed hands tagged by the Milwaukee County medical examiner as 'Hands C'. Eventually, his complete skeletal remains were discovered. At autopsy, Turner was identified from 'frozen cervical and lumbar margins, bone marrow, hair from pelvis, skin pieces and right costal margin, oral and anal swabs, smears and saliva.' His father was notified of his son's death at 8.30 a.m. on 25 July 1991.

Jeremiah B. Weinberger

Born on 29 September 1967, Weinberger, of 3404 N. Halstead, Chicago, was reported missing by his father, David, to the Chicago PD on 6 July 1971. 'We're dealing with it as a family will deal with it,' said Mr Weinberger to press at the time. He was the long-time owner of Caffe Pergolesi, 3404 N. Halsted Street. 'We have a missing person in the family.'

Dahmer was back in Chicago again. Five days after killing Turner he was out looking for another victim. After visiting a gay club on Wells Street, Jeff went to Carol's, a seedy bar, and here he met twenty-three-year-old Weinberger and invited him back to Milwaukee. Weinberger asked a friend and former roommate, Ted Jones, whether he should accept. 'Sure, he looks okay,' said Jones. He was later to comment ruefully, 'Who knows what a serial killer looks like?'

Dahmer and Weinberger spent Saturday in apartment 213 having sex. Jeff appeared to like his new acquaintance but, the following day, when Weinberger looked at the clock and said it was time to go, Dahmer offered him a drink. Victim number fifteen went out like a light. Out came the camera – *flash flash flash*. Instead of using acid, Dahmer injected boiling water into Weinberger's skull, which left the lad in a zombie-like state for nearly two days. After using him to his liking, Dahmer then strangled him. His body was dismembered, and the remains dissolved in sulphuric acid. The head was placed on a shelf in the freezer.

Jeremiah's identification was found in Dahmer's apartment after his arrest. His complete skeletal remains were identified as a match. His father was notified of his son's death by the Chicago PD on 25 July 1991.

Oliver Joseph Lacy

Oliver, born on 23 June 1967 and residing at 3237 N. 24th Place, Milwaukee in 1991, had been missing since 12 July when his fiancée contacted police. He was eventually identified through his fingerprints which were obtained from severed hands that had been tagged by the Milwaukee County medical examiner as 'Hands A'. Oliver was not known to Milwaukee police. His recently-widowed mother was notified of his death on 24 July 1991, at 10.00 a.m.

His high school track coach, Glenn Cothern spoke to the *Chicago Tribune* in July 1991, saying that he was a 'young man who had his ups and downs in high school and afterward, yet Lacy seemed to be getting his life in order.' He was a sprinter on the Oak Park River High School's 1987 state championship track team. His coach was quick to praise Lacy saying that: 'Several times in his senior year he ran the hundred metre dash in ten and a half seconds – exceptional time for high school ... and there were no flukes about it.' Oliver was offered a track scholarship to Texas A&M University, but his grades were not high enough, so he attended a junior college to improve his grades. 'He was really trying to make something of himself,' Cothern remembered.

Lacy had moved from Chicago to Milwaukee earlier in July to be with his twenty-three-year-old fiancée, Rose Colon, and their two-year-old child, Emmanuel, and were living with Oliver's mother, Catherine Lacy in her duplex on Milwaukee's West Side. Oliver was a handsome young man who could have been a model. He'd got a job as custodian working in downtown for Pioneer Commercial Cleaning Inc. He was last seen on 12 July at the Grand Avenue Mall where he had gone with a friend at about 6 p.m. 'When he wasn't home Saturday, I felt something was wrong because my son would call me. My children always call me, and I also have another son and daughter,' Catherine told a reporter. She was adamant that she had no clue as to how Oliver was 'lured away' to his death. The lad didn't use drugs and had never engaged in homosexual activity. This was confirmed by high school friend, Iran Harris, who further said that Lacy had many female admirers.

Dahmer's account of what had happened to Oliver was that on 15 July he'd encountered Lacy at the corner of N. 27th Street and West Kilbourn Avenue just a few blocks from Dahmer's place.

Dahmer was extremely plausible, and he would have flattered Lacy about his 'model looks'. Therefore, it's more than plausible to suggest that Lacy, feeling at ease, agreed to Dahmer's offer of posing naked for photographs – in return for fifty bucks, of course.

Dahmer later told police that they had 'engaged in sexual activity'. It seems unlikely that, if this happened, the activity was consensual as Lacy's family and friends had never seen or guessed at any homosexual tendencies. Dahmer drugged Lacy and told police that he had intended to prolong the time he spent with the 'beautiful boy'. After unsuccessfully attempting to render Lacy unconscious with chloroform, he telephoned his workplace to request a day's absence. This was granted, although by now his employer had had enough of Dahmer's slack work record, so he was suspended shortly thereafter. After strangling Lacy, Dahmer had sex with the corpse before dismembering it. He placed the head and heart in his refrigerator, intending to consume it later. The skeleton was stuffed into the freezer. Four days later, on 19 July, Dahmer was fired by Ambrosia.

Joseph Bradehoft

'He [Dahmer] has many serious problems both emotionally and physically that need to be addressed.'

Donna Chester, Dahmer's probation officer

Dahmer's murder spree was almost over. Four days after killing Lacy, the head of the final victim joined the others in the freezer. He was twenty-five-year-old Joseph Bradehoft, an out-of-work African-American man who was hoping to move from Minnesota to Milwaukee.

With no job and no wages, Dahmer was now in a state of total decline. Poverty was nipping at his heels. He was also on the verge of eviction from his stinking apartment full of rotting body parts and bleached bones. He complained to his probation officer Donna Chester. He falsely told her that he had been absent from work because he had to look after his sick grandmother over in West Allis. He had been to visit her in hospital, he said, that because of this he had overslept, and he had been drinking too. 'That's why my boss unfairly sacked me,' he whined.

But just as the bosses at Ambrosia had become sick and tired of Dahmer's shoddy work output and sloppy attitude, Donna Chester was now also at the end of her tether too. She had been trying to get Dahmer on the straight and narrow for months. She had gone well beyond the call of duty with the young man whom she knew to be an out-and-out pathological liar through and through. Even though he was still seeing psychiatrists, Dahmer, it seemed, was determined to self-destruct.

Dahmer was often going unwashed and unshaven for days on end and he was frequently seen on 2nd Street, an industrial area with a scattering of homosexual bars. Robert Grunwald recalls 'He [Jeff] was the ultimate loner. He didn't move on people. He sat there quietly in the Wreck Room bar, watching.' Witness Michael Stocke said that he'd observed Dahmer enter another bar, order a screwdriver 'and sometimes simply stare straight ahead,' adding, 'he was very loud about being quiet. It was the demeanour of the man ... we were not sure that he belonged in a gay bar at all.' Actually, no one can recall Dahmer leaving a bar with someone. When he made his approach it was outside, where young men, some barely out of their teens, often loitered.

Donna Chester had by now filled her log with references to Dahmer's depression, financial problems and his difficulty in resolving his sexual identity. Her work with Dahmer had started way back on 15 February 1989, when he was still in a work release programme after the conviction for sexual assault of a child. Donna had the patience of a saint. In late April through May 1991, Donna Chester recalls that Dahmer was often unshaven and had dark circles beneath his eyes. He told her that police had questioned him about a man found strangled on the third floor of his building. (This case is still unsolved.) On 27 May, Jeff seems to have changed his tune and told Chester that he had no major problems. Still she noted in her log that 'he continues to complain about everything ... a chronic complainer ... always talking about committing suicide.'

One might say that Dahmer was once again at his 'Last Chance Saloon'. Donna urged him to come downtown to her office immediately, and perhaps something could be salvaged with his job. She could call the union representative at Ambrosia and try to get Jeff's job back. Dahmer refused, saying that he wasn't presentable – he had not shaved, nor taken a bath for three days. 'Come in anyway, Jeff,' Donna pleaded, and although he agreed, he failed to show up. As Don Davis says in his book, 'Dahmer had now reached a critical mass. A Jeffrey Dahmer with a job had been bad enough. Without one he had no anchors at all, but he did have a lot of anger. A whole mountain of it. And the mountain fell on Joseph Bradehoft.'[17]

On Friday, 19 July, this mountain of anger, frustration and pent-up fury sat down on one of the brown leatherette seats of a local bus. Dahmer was mad as hell at Ambrosia. He was mad at the bus driver's constant stop-and-going again, and he didn't like being crammed in with all these black people at all. He didn't like the stick-on signs ordering him not to smoke on the fucking bus, not to play a radio or tape deck, not to fucking drink, not to litter, not to eat on this fucking bus... not to breathe... fart... Jesus Christ, and if you did, hey ya'll dudes, here is another sign saying that undercover cops ride on the buses to keep an eye on things.

Can you see Jeff Dahmer now? I can. There's steam coming out of his ears. 'Enough of this shit,' Jeff is thinking, 'I'm outta this stinking bus with its sticky rubber floor under my shoes.' So he decided to hop off at the next stop and walk. The double doors swish open. He steps off and there, right in front of him, stands the gift of a lifetime – a handsome young man carrying a six-pack of beer.

It was twenty-five-year-old, Joseph Bradehoft. He was in town looking for a job that would enable him to support his wife and three kids. So he accepted Dahmer's offer of ready money in exchange for nude photographs and willingly joined in oral sex in Dahmer's apartment. After that he was drugged with one of Jeff's special cocktails, then strangled with Jeff's favourite strap. Out came Jeff's camera – *flash, flash, flash*. Joseph was dismembered, his body placed in a barrel of acid which was swiftly turned into a black, sticky mess. 'I froze some of the meat to eat at my own convenience,' Dahmer recalled later.

It remains baffling why the complaints of Dahmer's neighbours weren't sounding more alarm bells. Pamela Bass, one of Dahmer's neighbours, recalled later how bizarre and frankly disturbing life was at the Oxford Apartments during those days:

> 'I was trying to comprehend what was going on because how could he be doing all this kind of stuff right over here... right in the midst of us. Many senior citizens, people like me who is

befriending you and you are over here cutting up human bodies, eating body parts. I've eaten a sandwich from you. I've probably eaten someone's body parts. How dare you do this to me ... Penises, and there are boxes with penises in, and pictures of penises.'

Tracy Edwards

'This freak, this crazy guy was trying to hurt me.'

Panic stricken Tracy Edwards to police after escaping from Dahmer

Milwaukee is one of the most pleasant cities in the American Midwest. With wide avenues, a fine harbour on Lake Michigan, it is a city created by wealth. It is also one of the most ethnically and culturally diverse cities in the U.S.

The etymology – if you are into etymologies – of 'Milwaukee' comes from an Algonquian word *'millioke'*, meaning 'good', 'beautiful' and 'pleasant land'. The name, however, has a less pleasant connotation in the Menominee language, where it is called *Māēnāēwah*, meaning 'some misfortune happens', and by gosh some misfortune happened in one of the seedier districts along the tree-lined 25th Street, Milwaukee. A place with eighty-two per cent of the population consisting of underprivileged, low-income black and Asian people. And, back in Dahmer's day, most of the people who lived there rented one-room

184

apartments for under $300 a month. This is the area we have come to know as Dahmer's hunting grounds. With its boarded-up stores and strip joints the area had a high level of crime. It was also home to the gay community who were, in the nineties, still very much living on the margins of society – especially in a city run by a police force so drenched in homophobia.

So now, all Hell was about to break loose. It was 11.30 p.m., 22 July 1991. In the patrol car that is cruising along 25th, officers Robert Rauth and Rolf Mueller were looking forward to getting off duty in thirty minutes. The heat was oppressive and the humidity almost unbearable. The smell of the neighbourhood was more pungent in the heat – the reeking fly-blown garbage on the sidewalks, the urine and faeces left by the homeless, the stink of cooked grease. Suddenly there was a cry of 'Help!' that made them brake to a screeching halt. A short, slim black man was running towards them from the direction of the very high crime area around Marquette University. Handcuffs were hanging from his left wrist. His relief when he saw the police car was almost hysterical and the tale he babbled out sounded so extraordinary that the officers found it difficult to follow what he said. He tells them that a madman had tried to kill him and that the man had a knife. 'This freak, this crazy guy was trying to hurt me,' he said. 'He put his head on my chest … was listening to my heart … he said he was going to eat my heart.'

The officers sly-winked at each other and wearily climbed out of their car. The terrified man gave his name as Tracy Edwards and his age, thirty-two. Edwards led the cops to the white two-storey building called Oxford Apartments. Edwards told the officers that his attacker lived in apartment 213. The cops used the outside intercom, telling the man who answered it that they were police, which seems to indicate that they were not taking the matter very seriously. Dahmer released the front door lock and the cops, with Edwards in tow, entered. Can you see Jeff Dahmer now? Because I can. One might expect that he would have been shitting bricks... What do you think?

Jeffrey Dahmer gave the police his name. He looked gaunt and unwashed. He didn't smell too good either. As he politely stood aside to let them in, he seemed perfectly calm, looking dumbly at Edwards as if he'd never seen him before. At this point, both officers had a gut feeling that this was a false alarm – that was until their coppers' noses smelled the unpleasant odour of decay which pervaded the entire apartment.

When the officers asked why he had threatened Tracy Edwards, Jeff looked contrite, and explained that he had just lost his job and had been drinking. It was only a lovers' tiff he said. When the officers asked him for the key to the handcuffs, Dahmer looked nervous and tried to stall. 'Wait a moment,' he said, 'it's in the bedroom. I'll try and find it.' One of the cops decided to accompany him. In the bedroom he spotted the knife Edwards had mentioned and – more than that – he noticed photos lying around. The photos looked like they were of dismembered bodies. When he'd collected his wits he yelled for his partner. 'Cuff him!' Dahmer – who had until now presented as a quiet, placid man – suddenly became violent and hysterical. A beast was emerging from within.

A brief struggle ensued as the cops and Dahmer wrestled. Another resident heard one of the police officers say: 'The son of a bitch scratched me.' Moments later, Dahmer was face down on the floor in handcuffs. His Miranda Rights were being read to him as the cops' on-duty time expired – they were now earning overtime bonuses and it would be a long night too. Rauth called headquarters on his portable radio, requesting a criminal record check on Dahmer, then asked for back-up. The details came back quickly: Dahmer had a felony conviction for sexual assault and for assaulting a thirteen-year-old boy.

This all supported the story that Edwards – now able to speak calmly – went on to tell. He was a recent arrival in Milwaukee from Mississippi. It had started out all innocent enough that pleasant Monday evening when Tracy and some friends encountered this tall white guy as they hung out at the busy Grand Avenue shopping complex downtown. Tracy was acquainted with Dahmer – he'd seen him around – so he did not feel threatened in the least by him. And so the group readily agreed when he suggested that they go back to his apartment. He would pay the guys $100 to pose naked for photographs and they could 'soak up some beers.'

'The two of us will buy the drinks and ya'll can come by later,' Dahmer told Edwards' cronies, conveniently giving them a phony address. Edwards, it transpired, bought the beer. Dahmer and Edwards got into a taxi, made the quick trip up Wisconsin Avenue, turning right on N.25th until they stopped about two blocks from Oxford Apartments

– a ploy always used by Dahmer so no one would know where he lived.

Back at Dahmer's apartment, Edwards didn't like the stench, nor the male pin-ups on the walls. 'Jeff was a nice kindly person when he picked me up,' recalls Edwards, 'but the minute I stepped into the apartment there was like a foul odour in the room. I almost gagged.' Tracy wasn't gay and thought he was just there to keep Jeff company. But he was fascinated by Dahmer's fish tank containing Siamese fighting fish. Dahmer whispered in Tracy's ear: ' I love watching them fighting... the combat usually ends up with one of *them* dead... Let's have a drink of beer on the settee... your buddies will be here soon.'

Edwards was now a bit concerned. There were a couple of boxes of hydrochloric acid on the floor close by. Dahmer stated that he needed them for heavy-duty cleaning. Tracy kept looking at his watch. He'd expected his pals to have arrived by now. The smell in the apartment was becoming more pervasive. Dahmer kept looking at him in a very unsettling, creepy sort of way. When the beer was finished, Dahmer handed Edwards a rum-and-coke. The movement of the fighting fish was oddly hypnotic, and he was beginning to feel drowsy and high. Can you place yourself in Tracy's place right now – okay, best not then!

For some reason Dahmer kept asking him how he was feeling. But when Dahmer put his arms around him and whispered a suggestion about bed, Edwards was instantly awake. This was a mega mistake because, before he could react, he felt the cold steel of a handcuff bracelet clamped tightly around his wrist. Tracy began to struggle and prevented Dahmer from securing the other. Edwards then froze as his manic host pressed a six-inch butcher's knife to his chest, pricking him above his heart and in the groin, the once-amicable face of the white man now contorted into a terrifying mask of hatred and hell-bent fury.

'His face was *completely* changed,' Tracy later told police. 'I wouldn't have recognised him. It was as if the devil himself stood in front of me. Then he said in a chilling way with precise instructions: "You die if you don't do what I say".'

Edwards obeyed.

Dahmer later told police that what he wanted to see was the 'body of the trim black man, a body that had been kept lean through manual labor.' Edwards, knowing he was in danger, tried for a time to remain unthreatening and appease his host. To buy some time, he tried a bit of seduction, slowly unbuttoning his own shirt from the top. This must have been terrifying as he simultaneously took in the nauseating smell of the room and gazed upon the sickening amateur shots that showed dismembered bodies and chunks of meat that looked like joints in a butcher's shop. Tracy thought that much of the stench came from a blue, plastic barrel with a black lid that stood under a part-open window. By now, Tracy could make a good guess as to what it contained. Tracy Edwards played Dahmer perfectly. For four hours he teased, suggested and posed for Dahmer, 'dancing very carefully on the edge of a madman's razor-sharp knife,'[18] as author Don Davis so eloquently describes.

One important thing that I have learned throughout my lengthy career interviewing sexual psychopaths is that they often *imagine* they are in control when, in actuality, they are not. Their over-inflated ego is the thing that most often prevents them from seeing reality. In this instance, I think that Dahmer believed that he was in control. He had always been in control. He had outwitted the 'system' time and again. Now he felt emboldened once more with a handsome, young, muscular, black body, which he *believed* was at his complete disposal. He announced that it was time to go to bed, so they went to the bedroom.

By now, although still terrified, Tracy was getting inside Dahmer's head. He asked Jeff if, before they made love, they could settle down and watch a film. Jeff fell for the ploy and suggested *The Exorcist III* – the 1990 psychological horror movie and sequel to the infamous film of the same name – that depicts a priest possessed by the devil. 'He was chanting and rocked back and forth and becoming over-excited during some of the scenes,' recalled Tracy. 'I tried to calm him down because he said that he was afraid of being disliked and left alone.'

At this point in the morbid scheme of things, it might be worthwhile trying to think as Dahmer might have done as he, and the handsome Tracy, sat-close-up-and-personal-together on the couch. Jeff's warped sexual psychopathology...let's say his fantasy-loved-up-world... to keep Tracy...cuddled up to him every night...to share their lives as real lovers in the real world, but... with Jeff living in a world where pink elephants fly, lead balls bounce and fairies reign supreme – in marketing terms this was a 'Loss Leader' in every event, *et al.*

So, do we recall his entire narrative almost from age four through to the psychiatric findings of the doctors/

psychiatrists who examined Dahmer many times later – of course we do? Can we say it that 'clusterfuck throughout' applies right until RIGHT NOW, as Dahmer, without a dime to his name, eviction from his apartment on the cards, has finally entered his 'Last Chance Saloon'… and he gets it too.

Tracy Edwards was also getting the picture by now. A picture that involved multiple dead men, decapitated heads, carved up corpses, blood and severed hands. Something was inside that blue barrel. He had to escape – but how? To pacify Dahmer even more, he repeatedly pledged that he was his friend and that he wasn't going to run away. All the while he was glancing across at the open window. Perhaps, if it came down to it, Tracy could take a leap of faith? But that leap might have broken his neck, back and legs. He then asked Dahmer if they could grab some beer in the living room where there was air conditioning. The serial killer consented. Maybe it was out of excited anticipation, but Dahmer seems to have had a momentary lapse of concentration in this case, which proved to be Edwards's miraculous opportunity. As Edwards rose from the couch, he turned and punched Dahmer squarely in the face. This move stunned the Milwaukee Cannibal momentarily, allowing Edwards to run for his life. He raced out of the front door, dashed down the stairs and sprinted a few blocks before finally flagging down the two cops.

Tracy Edwards had survived his encounter with Jeffrey Dahmer and, in doing so, had brought his monstrous series of murders to a close. Edwards did not have a happy ending though. He was in and out of trouble with the police for years and remained homeless, moving from shelter to shelter. He suffered from addictions to drugs and alcohol. In 2011 he was arrested and convicted of homicide after another homeless man was thrown from the Milwaukee Bridge.

The Abattoir

'You think you've seen it all.'

MPD Officer Rolf Mueller, a ten-year police veteran
and one of the officers who arrested Jeffrey Dahmer

With Jeffrey Dahmer in cuffs, with back-up on the way,
MPD officers Robert Rauth and Rolf Mueller started to
look around the dingy, fly-infested small one-bedroomed
apartment. Some electrical power tools lay over by the
sofa. Dozens more Polaroid photos of dismemberment
were scattered around and there was a large, dried
bloodstain that mottled the bed. The stench of the place
made them gag. Officer Mueller opened the refrigerator
and Lacy's severed head stared straight back at him. He
shrieked loudly: 'There's a freakin' head in this fridge!' and
he slammed the door shut.

While the place was neat and relatively clean, especially for
a bachelor, the smell of decomposition was overwhelming.
The bathroom door was fitted with a deadbolt lock. In
the closet was a metal stockpot containing decomposing

hands and a penis. On the shelf were two skulls. Also in the closet were containers of ethyl alcohol, chloroform and formaldehyde, along with some glass jars containing more genitalia preserved in formaldehyde. The photos showed Dahmer's many victims at various stages of death – one of a man's head, the flesh still intact, lying in a sink. Another photo displayed a victim cut from the neck to the groin like a deer gutted after the kill. The cut was so clean one could clearly see the pelvic bone. Some of the photos were of his victims before he murdered them – striking erotic or bondage poses. Police would later learn that Dahmer had had sex with all of the corpses and masturbated over them. As for the skulls – he masturbated in front of them for sexual gratification too.

Inquisitive neighbours would soon tell the investigators that for more than a year they had complained repeatedly of a stench from the apartment. They also had heard the sound of sawing at all hours. A hazardous-materials team wearing yellow rubber suits and breathing from air tanks arrived to begin removing the boxes of body parts, a barrel of acid, the refrigerator containing the head, and the dresser brimming with photos and drawings of mutilated dead bodies. The area around the Oxford Apartments began to fill with police vehicles of every kind. Detectives in sports jackets, officers in blue uniforms, officials from the coroner's office and the District Attorney's office rushed to the scene – followed in hot pursuit by the media. Newspaper reporters and film crews from TV stations with floodlights that illuminated the place like some macabre circus filled the streets. Police Chief Phillip Arreola was up front batting away most of the questions. All he would say was that they were investigating the murder of fifteen plus victims who were 'male and of various races'.

The first items of evidence came by way of a literal head-count: seven skulls and four heads that still had flesh on them. The gore was overwhelming. Next to Lacy's head, on the bottom shelf of the fridge, was an open box of baking soda to help soak up the odour of decomposition. The fridge's upper freezer compartment contained some 'unidentified meat' in plastic bags, including something identified as a human heart. In the lower freezer, three more heads were found, enclosed in garbage bags and tied with plastic twists.

In a corner of the bedroom, inside a box that had previously held Dahmer's Myoda laptop computer, were two skulls and an album full of the dreadful pictures he'd taken when gutting his human prey. Beside it, under the window was the large fifty-five-gallon blue barrel that Tracy Edwards had noticed. Underneath its black lid, it was jammed with body parts and bones all fizzing away in acid. A filing cabinet beside the bed had two drawers which contained three skulls and a jumble of human bones. Several of the skulls had been painted grey so that they looked similar to the plastic replica skulls that are sold at carnivals and gift shops. Upon opening the bedroom closet, investigators found a kettle on the top shelf. In it were more human artefacts. Another kettle was removed from the bottom of the closet and inside were a genital organ and some human hands.

The full inventory of items and description of evidence seized in Dahmer's apartment is, courtesy of the Federal Bureau of Investigation, 10th Street & Pennsylvania Avenue.,

N.W. Washington, D.C., can be found in Appendix A of this book.

*

Three days after his arrest, on Thursday, 25 July 1991, Jeffrey Dahmer – represented by Gerald P. Boyle and Wendy Patrickus – was brought before the court. Unshaven, with a dark, two-day growth of stubble on his chin and dark rings encircling his puffy eyes, he was named in a criminal complaint that accused him of four counts of first-degree homicide.

As with certain other provisions of Wisconsin's criminal code, the ways in which state law defines homicide charges are somewhat unique. Technically speaking, there is no crime of 'murder' in 'The Badger State'. Instead, the offence commonly referred to as murder in other states is classified as 'intentional homicide' in Wisconsin. If perchance you have thought about killing someone in Wisconsin – which I am sure you are not – under Section 940.01 of the Wisconsin Statutes, first-degree intentional homicide is defined as: 'Caus[ing] the death of another human being [or an unborn child] with intent to kill that person or another.' I am raising this issue here because it is true to say that the term 'homicide' can actually mean something slightly different to the word 'murder'. It classifies the 'manner of death'. For example, if we looked at the killing of forty-six-year-old George Perry Floyd Jr, by thuggish Minneapolis cop Derek Chauvin on 25 May 2020. In this case, the medical examiner stated, as a witness at trial that Mr Floyd's manner of death was 'homicide' in a *medical* sense and not in the *legal* sense. So, if you can get your head round that then you win a yet unspecified prize, because you are a better man/woman than I am.

First-degree intentional homicide in Wisconsin is a Class A felony, which carries the potential for life imprisonment. The death penalty in Wisconsin was abolished in 1853 and was one of the earliest states to abolish the punishment.

The initial court proceedings entailed an Affidavit filed by Homicide Lt. David Kane, all of which detailed what had occurred when Officers Rauth and Mueller first entered the apartment at 925 N. 25th Street. Lt. Kane also noted the Medical Examiner's initial findings given by Jeffrey Jentzen, so County Circuit Judge Frank T. Crivello approved the motion that Dahmer be denied bail because he could not stump up the one million dollars District Attorney Edward Michael McCann demanded.

CRIMINAL COMPLAINT

In the State of Wisconsin, Plaintiff, verses Jeffrey L. Dahmer, Defendant. Complaining Witness Donald Domagalski, being duly sworn, says that the above-named defendant in the County of Milwaukee, State of Wisconsin:

COUNT 01: FIRST DEGREE MURDER

in January of 1988, at 2357 South 57th Street, City of West Allis, County of Milwaukee, did cause the death of another human being, James E. Doxtator, with intent to kill that person contrary to Wisconsin Statutes section 940.01.

COUNT 02: FIRST DEGREE MURDER

in March of 1988, at 2357 South 57th Street, City of West Allis, County of Milwaukee, did cause the death of another human being, Richard Guerrero, with intent to kill that person contrary to Wisconsin Statutes section 940.01.

COUNT 03: FIRST DEGREE INTENTIONAL HOMICIDE

on or about March 26, 1989, at 2357 South 57th Street, City of West Allis, County of Milwaukee, did cause the death of another human being, Anthony Sears, with intent to kill that person contrary to Wisconsin Statutes section 940.01(1).

COUNT 04: FIRST DEGREE INTENTIONAL HOMICIDE

during the Spring or early Summer of 1990, at 924 North 25th Street, City and County of Milwaukee, did cause the death of another human being, Raymond Smith a/k/a Ricky Beeks, with intent to kill that person contrary to Wisconsin Statutes section 940.01(1).

COUNT 05: FIRST DEGREE INTENTIONAL HOMICIDE

during the Summer of 1990, at 924 North 25th Street, City and County of Milwaukee, did cause the death of another human being, Edward W. Smith, with intent to kill that person contrary to Wisconsin Statutes section 940.01(1).

COUNT 06: FIRST DEGREE INTENTIONAL HOMICIDE

on or about September 3, 1990, at 924 North 25th Street, City and County of Milwaukee, did cause the death of another human being, Ernest Miller, with intent to kill that person contrary to Wisconsin Statutes section 940.01(1).

COUNT 07: FIRST DEGREE INTENTIONAL HOMICIDE

on or about September 24, 1990, at 924 North 25th Street, City and County of Milwaukee, did cause the death of another human being, David Thomas, with intent to kill that person contrary to Wisconsin Statutes section 940.01(1).

COUNT 08: FIRST DEGREE INTENTIONAL HOMICIDE

on or about February 18, 1991, at 924 North 25th Street, City and County of Milwaukee, did cause the death of another human being, Curtis Straughter, with intent to kill that person contrary to Wisconsin Statutes section 940.01(1).

COUNT 09: FIRST DEGREE INTENTIONAL HOMICIDE

on or about April 7, 1991, at 924 North 25th Street, City and County of Milwaukee, did cause the death of another human being, Errol Lindsey, with intent to kill that person contrary to Wisconsin Statutes section 940.01(1).

COUNT 10: FIRST DEGREE INTENTIONAL HOMICIDE

on or about May 24, 1991, at 924 North 25th Street, City and County of Milwaukee, did cause the death of another human being, Tony Anthony Hughes, with intent to kill that person contrary to Wisconsin Statutes section 940.01(1).

COUNT 11: FIRST DEGREE INTENTIONAL HOMICIDE

on or about May 27, 1991, at 924 North 25th Street, City and County of Milwaukee, did cause the death of another human being, Konerak Sinthasomphone, with intent to kill that person contrary to Wisconsin Statutes section 940.01(1).

COUNT 12: FIRST DEGREE INTENTIONAL HOMICIDE

on or about June 30, 1991, at 924 North 25th Street, City and County of Milwaukee, did cause the death of another human being, Matt Turner a/k/a Donald Montrell, with intent to kill that person contrary to Wisconsin Statutes section 940.01(1).

COUNT 13: FIRST DEGREE INTENTIONAL HOMICIDE

on or about July 7, 1991, at 924 North 25th Street, City and County of Milwaukee, did cause the death of another human being, Jeremiah Weinberger, with intent to kill that person contrary to Wisconsin Statutes section 940.01(1).

COUNT 14: FIRST DEGREE INTENTIONAL HOMICIDE

on or about July 15, 1991 at 924 North 25th Street, City and County of Milwaukee, did cause the death of another human being, Oliver Lacy, with intent to kill that person contrary to Wisconsin Statutes section 940.01(1).

COUNT 15: FIRST DEGREE INTENTIONAL HOMICIDE

on or about July 19, 1991 at 924 North 25th Street, City and County of Milwaukee, did cause the death of another human being, Joseph Bradehoft, with intent to kill that person contrary to Wisconsin Statutes section 940.01(1).

On the advice of his defence team – Boyle and Patrickus – Dahmer pleaded guilty, but he also pleaded insanity. The prosecution, led by DA McCann, refused to accept the insanity plea. The state pointed out that if Dahmer were found guilty but insane he could plead for a review of his case after two years. Theoretically he might then be released. This was, admittedly, unlikely – but still it was legally on the cards. And, at this place would you, reader, use your own common sense to determine whether you think Jefferey Dahmer was mad, bad or sad?

Enter the Psychiatrists

'This is the kid who got his hand caught in the cookie jar.
Now, not everyone kills when they get their hand caught in
the cookie jar. But Jeffrey Dahmer found that that was the
easy way out. And so he killed. My feeling was that he had
created this situation where the easy way out was to destroy
that person, and therefore, there would be nobody out there
in the community that could come back and say "Jeffrey
Dahmer is a homosexual".'

Judge Laurence C. Gram Jr., *Tampa Bay Times*, 11 October 2005

Charged with fifteen counts of first-degree homicide,
Dahmer's trial started on 30 January 1992 before devout
Catholic, Judge Laurence C. 'Larry' Gram Jr.. Gram
decided that there was no way he was going to allow the
hearings to turn into a 'media circus'. Judge Gram was
regarded as a middle-of-the-road jurist who came down
hard on sex offenders and drug dealers. 'I'm a judge
twenty-four hours a day, seven-days a week, 365 days a
year,' Gram said. 'I take this pretty seriously.'

By previously pleading guilty on 13 January, Dahmer had waived his rights to an initial trial to establish guilt (as defined in Wisconsin Law). The sole issue of the trial – one which would become the subject of heated debate by opposing counsels and their respective shrinks – was to determine whether Dahmer suffered from either a mental or a personality disorder. In short, it was to establish whether he was sane. The prosecution claimed that any such disorders did not deprive Dahmer of the ability to appreciate the criminality of his conduct, or to deprive him of the ability to resist his impulses. The defence, on the other hand, argued that their client suffered from a mental disease and was driven by obsessions and impulses that he was unable to control. In a nutshell (s'cuse the pun) to substantiate an insanity defence one has to establish that the M'Naghten Rule applies. Under Wisconsin law the Universal Citation is: WI Stat § 971.15 (2013 through Act 380):

> '... that every man is to be presumed sane, and ... that to establish a defence on the grounds of insanity, it must be clearly proved that, at the time of the committing of the act, the party accused was labouring under such a defect of reason, from disease of the mind, as not to know the nature and quality of the act he was doing; or if he did know it, that he did not know he was doing what was wrong.'

The subject and the debates surrounding the M'Naghten Rule (pronounced, and often spelled, McNaughton), could fill a thousand books. It has been a perpetual cause of disagreement amongst courtroom forensic psychiatrists in the US since it was established in the 1840s whenever an insanity defence is offered by way of mitigation, especially in cases of murder most foul. It's a question that this book attempts to answer: did Jeff Dahmer know the difference between right and wrong? Was he cognitively up-to-speed? And was he able to control his behaviour and conform to the law?

Throughout this book I have referred to the 'waypoints' in every person's narrative: times, locations and circumstances where decisions are made as to which path to take. Therefore, along our *own* journey thus far – with you dear reader most certainly getting to know Mr Dahmer much better than most – can you say that *he didn't know* what he was doing was wrong... as in *very wrong*? You might ask yourself: did he not try and cover his murderous tracks over a considerable period of time? Did he not go out to gay bars and other places with murder a forethought in his mind? And, was he not fully aware that drugging young men, drilling holes into their skulls and injecting acid or boiling water while they were still alive was not only illegal but amoral, unlawful and downright sickening? Any psychiatrist who claims that monsters like Dahmer have no clue as to what they are up to needs their own head examined too. Would you disagree?

How often do the guilty walk free and how often are the innocent incarcerated? After examining every capital punishment case passing through the appeal courts between 1973 and 1995, lawyers at the Columbian School of Law in New York found that seven out of ten death sentences were reversed because of serious error in the original trials. In over sixty per cent of the cases, psychiatric evaluations had played no small role in the original proceedings.

Psychiatry and psychology are 'inexact sciences' for want of a better term. The practitioners of these two *specific* disciplines form 'professional opinions' often invested with great integrity. However this integrity is often ill-founded; their opinions having been coloured by predisposition towards their own favoured ideals and disciplines. They are often less-equipped to penetrate the criminal mind than others.

Out of court, and visiting the accused in a prison environment, psychiatrists are often in total disagreement among themselves when judging the state of an accused's mind. This 'professional' in-fighting that has often led to disastrous and tragic results. The cases are legion, and each one brings its own irreparable aftermath. So, when I consider Dahmer's state of mind and the insanity plea, the case that immediately springs to mind if that of Arthur John Shawcross (1945-2008). This serial killer – whom I interviewed on camera at the Sullivan Correctional Facility, Fallsburg, New York – was given a derisory twenty-five-year prison sentence after pleading guilty to two counts of first-degree manslaughter of eight-year-old Karen Ann Hill and ten-year-old Jack Owen Blake. Shawcross raped and murdered Jack in May 1972 but his body was not found until September in woodland. Just days before that discovery Shawcross snatched Karen, raped and murdered her. He was arrested the next day. It was argued by the District Attorney that, as there was no evidence linking him to Jack Blake's murder, Shawcross should be able to plead manslaughter for both deaths. In the case of Shawcross, it was less of a search for the truth than the pursuit of a quick plea-bargain deal, intended to save the State the cost of a fully-blown murder trial. This strategy would backfire horribly.

Shawcross – like so many of the thirty or so serial killers, mass-murderers and spree/rampage killers I have interviewed – was a master manipulator. Like Dahmer, 'Art' was nobody's fool and, not unlike thousands of other felons, he knew that the probable key to a successful parole application lay in appealing to the sensibilities of the welfare authorities, the prison psychiatrists and the church. Initially, whilst being held at the Green Haven Correctional Facility and to the delight of a few resident psychiatrists, Shawcross was to be found exhibiting all the welcome traits of a 'reformed man'. He started attending religious services – although previously he had never entered a church in his life. He conned his way into a counsellor's job in the prison's mental health unit. Here, he learned the language of psychology and psychiatry and persuaded psychiatrists to support his parole application.

Dissenting from the opinions of his colleagues, Green Haven psychiatrists, Dr Robert Kemp had formed the opinion that 'Shawcross would possibly be the most dangerous individual to be released into the community in years.' He was supported by his colleague Dr Y.A. Haveiwala. Dr Haveiwala concluded that Shawcross was 'a grave parole risk with an antisocial personality disorder [sociopath] and schizoid personality disorder with psychosexual conflicts.'

Shawcross's prison records show a hotchpotch of so-called professional interpretations laced with educated and uneducated guesswork. Yet, despite the alarmingly wide variance in 'qualified opinion' he was freed on April 30, 1987, ten years before his full twenty-five-year tariff had expired. During his first year of liberty, he killed again and again, and went on to leave a trail of another eleven bodies behind him. The psychiatrists at Green Haven CF kept their jobs.

Part of this blame for this carnage rests on the fact that Shawcross's first trial was rushed and allowing his plea bargain was motivated by the need to keep costs down. The cost of the lives extinguished by Shawcross is immeasurable. While a price cannot be placed on the degree of human suffering, the cost to the public purse *can* be defined, and the figures are truly astronomical. Aside from the $35,000 spent to bring Shawcross to 'justice' for the two earlier child murders, and the $250,000 to keep him at Green Haven CF and incidentals such as psychiatrists' bills before his early release, there is also the invoice for the later Rochester, NY, homicides to tally up. For this, aside from Shawcross himself, we can only blame several of the psychiatrists at Green Haven CF for concluding that he was safe to be released back into the community. The Rochester Police Department (RPD). conducted 2,210 interviews during the investigation into the murders committed by Shawcross. Around 3,255 licence plate inquiries were made at $12 a time as the police developed leads on 150 suspects. On-duty personnel costs add a further $420.447. Overtime costs were $121,916. Non-personnel services added $27,196. In total, these costs reached a staggering $608,619.

However, the Rochester Police Department add a rider to these figures, noting that the total would have been dramatically inflated – by perhaps an additional $2 million – if factors such as: patrol time/area altered to a specific pattern; training of investigative personnel, and volunteer hours spent on the investigation by RPD civilian employees were included. Finally, to keep Shawcross in prison until he was eighty-years-old (his sentence for the subsequent murders was 250 years), would cost the taxpayer a further £750,000 at the rates at that time.

When I interviewed the trial judge, His Honour Donald J. Wisner commented: 'The psychiatrists at Green Haven acted like Monday morning quarterbacks. It is a disgrace.' In response, Dr Kent replied: 'We just hate it when one of our people [Shawcross] goes sour.' Using just the single example above – and there are literally thousands more on public record let us ask a bold question. 'Do psychiatrists have a place in the courtroom?'

The court's role is primarily to establish guilt or innocence, to get to the truth of the case. Did 'A' shoot 'B', with this revolver? Either by admission of guilt, or through expert ballistic evidence, linked with a chain of strong circumstantial evidence, the fact is proven or not proven. In the Dahmer case, we ask: 'Did he commit all of the atrocious crimes he has admitted to?' The answer is, yes!

A trial is a contest between two sides, the prosecution and the defence, and each side having a team of players. And, invariably, each team might well employ the services of psychiatrists and psychologists to bolster their case. But why? They are not called to give evidence over material fact, or even concerned with the arithmetic of circumstantial evidence. They are called by their 'employers' – prosecution and defence – to give an 'opinion' as to the defendant's state of mind, prior to, during the commission of, and post-crime. As individuals, or as a small collective, these opinions are often demonstrated to be flawed. By the time flaws come to light, the consequences could be fateful. The defence might be seeking to influence a jury with mitigation of sentence in mind. The prosecution will be attempting to argue otherwise. Once the contest is in full swing, the jurors are drawn into nebulous and intangible concepts and issues. Quite often a jury is swayed by the testimony of a particularly eloquent or persuasive expert when the testimony is questionable.

During Dahmer's trial, the defence experts argued that their client was insane as evidenced by his necrophilia – his compulsion to have sexual encounters with the corpses of his victims. Dr Fred Berlin was hauled into court and testified that Dahmer was unable to conform his conduct at the time; that he committed the crimes because he was suffering from paraphilia or, more specifically, necrophilia. Next up for the defence was another expert witness, Dr Judith Becker, a professor of psychiatry and psychology, who also diagnosed Dahmer with necrophilia. Needless to say, a third 'expert witness' was called to testify on behalf of Dahmer's state of mind. Forensic psychiatrist Dr Carl Wahlstrom who acknowledged that Dahmer was a necrophile, but he added: borderline personality disorder; schizotypal personality disorder; alcohol dependence and a psychotic disorder. All heady stuff with lots of big labels but none of which fits the M'Naghten Rule cap, does it?

Dahmer originally claimed that he had no recollection of committing any of the murders – but this excuse had suddenly fallen by the wayside. Because it was clear that Dahmer recalled his crimes all too well. His police interviews proved that he had a remarkable memory for dates, places, circumstances and details about his victims, and what he did to them when he got them home. How can one forget about drilling a hole in some kid's head and injecting acid – I'd recall doing that wouldn't you? It's also obvious that Dahmer's defence team, forensic psychiatrists included, were on an uphill struggle from the get-go. And, the thing is they knew it. He's insane, they claimed. So the best place for Dahmer was a hospital for mentally ill people where, in a handful of years or so, a bunch of bickering doctors might well believe that – since he had returned to reality, was now a vegetarian or maybe even a vegan as he hadn't eaten any of the other patients while bouncing off of the walls – it would be safe, in their 'expert opinion' to set him free. But why even consider placing Dahmer into a mental hospital? He was a sado-sexual homicidal psychopath. No matter how many pills one made him swallow, psychopathy can never be cured.

But wait, help from the real world was at hand. The prosecution rejected the defence's argument that Jeffrey was insane. Forensic psychiatrist, Dr Phillip Resnick, testified that Dahmer, 'did not suffer from primary necrophilia because he preferred live sexual partners, as evidenced by his efforts to create unresisting, submissive sexual partners devoid of rational thought and to whose needs he did not have to cater.' But, Dr 'Phil', we must remind you that Jeffrey did, on many occasions, have sex with some of the corpses, did he not, which kind of throws the 'primary' part out of the window.

A Dr Fred Fosdel testified to his belief that Dahmer was 'without mental disease or defect at the time he committed the murders.' He went on to say that Dahmer was a 'calculating and cunning individual, able to differentiate between right and wrong, with the ability to control his actions.' Although Dr Fosdel agreed that Dahmer suffered from paraphilia, his conclusion was that Jeff was *not* a sadist. Quite where in Fosdel's *belief* came his conclusion that Dahmer was *not* a sadist remains to be seen. 'Sadism' is explicitly defined: 'as the tendency to derive pleasure, especially sexual gratification, from inflicting pain, suffering, or humiliation on others.' It is, of course a personality disorder, one often involving sadomasochism which appeared in an appendix of the *Diagnostic and Statistical Manual of Mental Disorders* (DSM-III-R) although later versions did not include it.

For the reader's edification, DSM-III-R is the must-read, must-go-to-reference for psychiatrists and psychologists worldwide. It's a sort of trainspotter's guide to every known mental illness or psychological disorder known to humanity. Trust me when I tell ya'll that DSM-II-R is *the* book for the dedicated trick cyclist, the couch head-shrinker, and just about every psychologist, psychoanalyst, psychotherapist who has ever been born and those yet to come. This is Freudian, Jungian, Alderian, Gestalt psychology Jack-off, hard-on literature. It's about intellect – to wit the absence of. The pages – and there are lots and lots of pages – are explicit about vacuity, brainlessness and up shit creek disordered moronic behavioural traits. It's all about what goes on inside one's grey matter you see, because the authors of DSM-II-R are well into lack of cognition, absence of perception even an active psychogenesis, *et al*, infinitum the science, or lack of science concerning the human mind, if you will?

And, herein sits a big problem. DSM-II-R is a bit like the *Holy Bible*. It's jam packed with contradiction. In the 'Good Book' we have 'An Eye for an Eye', then we get '... bear with each other and forgive one another if any of you has a grievance against someone'. This is why religion has caused more debate, incited more wars, than any book ever published, simply because people can't decide what is right or what is wrong, and you would not be alone in this thinking. For example, nip down to one's local tightwads Jehovah's Witnesses meetings. Get a freebee copy of *Watchtower*, then hightail it to one's nearest Anglican church – where they *do* give one tea, coffee, and biscuits – and you will, most certainly get a different take, more than likely some homemade cake, from the grey rinses of the knitting circle. And, this is why DSM-II-R is probably better employed as an item to prevent one's clinic door from shutting while Dr Shrink (USA only applies here) extracts as much money from his utterly neurotic patients as possible... And while you'll never find too many psychiatrists agreeing with each other in a court of law – period! More to the point, do we not see this taking place now as Mr Dahmer pleads his case – one of 'not guilty by reason of insanity' – when the shrinks who must, *or should at least* have filled their own minds with DSM-II-R. Yet they bicker, squabble and argue the toss in the sole interest of their own financial rewards and self-interest grandstanding kudos when appearing for either side.

It's difficult to see how anyone could agree with Dahmer's defence psychiatrists' premise that their client was insane for he would have had to have experienced pockets of insanity. For example, he could not have been said to be unaware of his own actions or purpose while he was stalking for prey in gay bars, working his job at the chocolate factory, telling half-truths and lies to family, his neighbours, his probation officer and the police who found him on the street with Konerak. Actually, I regard any such cock-and-bull psychiatric defence of 'temporary' if not 'fleeting insanity' as an utter slur to the grieving next-of-kin and indeed society as a whole. To argue temporary insanity for one crime would be worthy of consideration but Dahmer had murdered seventeen times. As for his claim that he had no memory of these crimes – the more than seventy polaroids that littered his home must have more than jogged his memory.

The final expert witness to appear for the prosecution, was forensic psychiatrist Park Dietz, and he began his testimony on 12 February. Dietz is a man who knows precisely what he is talking about, too. He has consulted or testified in many of the highest US criminal cases, including spousal killer Betty Broderick, mass murderer Jared Lee Loughner, and serial killers, Joel Rifkin, Arthur Shawcross, Richard Kuklinski aka 'The Unabomber', the Beltway sniper attacks (John Allen Muhammad and Lee Boyd Malvo), and William Bonin. He testified that he did not believe Dahmer to be suffering from any mental disease or defect at the time that he committed the crimes, stating: 'Dahmer went to great lengths to be alone with his victim and to have no witnesses.' He explained that there was ample evidence that the accused prepared in advance for each murder, concluding therefore, that his crimes were not impulsive. Although Park Dietz did concede any acquisition of a paraphilia was not a matter of personal choice, he also stated his belief that Dahmer's habit of becoming intoxicated prior to committing each of the murders was significant, stating: 'If he had an impulse to kill or a compulsion to kill, he wouldn't have to drink alcohol to overcome it. He only has to drink alcohol to overcome it because he is inhibited against killing.'

Park Dietz also noted that Dahmer strongly identified with evil and corrupt characters from both *The Exorcist III* and *Return of Jedi*; particularly the level of power held by these characters. Expounding on the significance of these movies in Dahmer's psyche and many of the murders committed in apartment 213, Dietz explained that the accused occasionally viewed scenes from these films before searching for a victim. Dietz concluded his testimony in diagnosing Dahmer with 'substance use disorder' (alcoholism), 'paraphilia' (an emotional disorder characterised by sexually arousing fantasies, urges, or behaviours that are recurrent, intense, occur over a period of at least six months, and cause significant distress or interfere with the sufferer's work, social function or other important areas of functioning), and 'schizotypal personality disorder'. (STPD is characterised by thought disorder, paranoia, a characteristic form of social anxiety, derealisation, transient psychosis, and unconventional beliefs).

During a filmed interview, Park Dietz recalled:

> 'I became Dahmer's confidante. I spent three days with him near to the judge's chambers; sometimes alone with him but always with law enforcement close by. He was not handcuffed, and I had no concern whatsoever. I was not his type, I guess.
>
> 'Jeffrey Dahmer was on a futile search for a placid, compliant, non-demanding sexual partner who would not leave him and he tried every maladjusted strategy to that goal... to achieve that. The one thing he never learned how to do was to find a consenting partner who liked to do the same things he did. For each of the homicides in Wisconsin, he tried to make sure no one saw him going home with the victim. If they went by cab they were dropped off at a different street a few blocks away so no-one could identify where Dahmer lived.'

Park Dietz was also interested in the types of movies Dahmer liked:

> 'As we watched several of his movies together I asked him to stop at parts that were significant to him. First, he stopped at several places which were particularly attractive to him... biceps, his favourite was biceps. But while watching some of the other movies, I was surprised at what he thought was sexual.

'One was in a *Star Wars* movie… that he thought Darth Vader's power was really sexy and appealing, and he wanted something to happen.'

When Park Dietz was asked why Dahmer took so many Polaroid photos, he replied:

'The soft tissue was all to be eliminated but he had hoped to retain some mementos of some of his crimes … What he hoped to keep without the risk of being caught were ten skulls and skeletons. You know, when I want to understand a killer, I want to see it from their point of view.'

To conclude the psychiatric testimony, two court-appointed mental health professionals testified independently of either prosecution or defence. There were forensic psychiatrist George B. Palermo and clinical psychologist Samuel H. Friedman. Palermo stated that the murders were the result of a 'pent-up aggression within himself [Dahmer]. He killed those men because he wanted to kill the source of his homosexual attraction to them. In killing them, he killed what he hated in himself.' Palermo concluded that Dahmer was a sexual sadist – which contradicted Dr Fred Fosdel's claim that Dahmer was *not* a sadist – with antisocial personality disorder, but legally sane. Samuel Friedman testified that it was a 'longing for companionship' that caused Dahmer to kill.

One might picture Judge Gram now overseeing this trial, muttering under his breath while peering over his wire-rimmed spectacles, having to listen to these highly-paid expert head-shrinkers who are not only contradicting each other but even themselves. In fact, the reader can try this for him or herself. Try 'sadism' for example. Go on give it a whirl, then tell me that Dr Fred Fosdel is correct, that Palermo is wrong; or that Palermo is right, and Fred hasn't yet understood that the Marquis de Sade was never a St. Agnes of Rome *aka* 'The Virgin and Patron Saint of Girls'. Friedman described Dahmer as: 'Amiable, pleasant to be with … courteous … with a sense of humour … conventionally in a ho-hum handsome and charming in manner … he's a bright young man.' However, Friedman went on to say that, in Dahmer, he saw 'a picture of a lonely, alienated small boy who has difficulty relating to anyone.' He ended his testimony by concluding that there was '*no* substance to Dahmer's insanity plea.'

Dahmer's trial lasted a fortnight. On 14 February, both counsels delivered their closing arguments to the jury. Each lawyer was allowed to speak for two hours, with defence attorney Gerald Boyle going first; repeatedly harking to the testimony of the mental health professionals from both camps – almost all of whom had agreed, disagreed or partly agreed – that Dahmer was suffering from a mental disease. Boyle argued that his client's compulsive killings had been the result 'of a sickness he discovered, not chose.' Boyle was canny and used Samuel Friedman's clinical playbook to portray Jeff as a 'desperately lonely and profoundly sick individual so out of control he could not conform his conduct anymore.' Ah, bless the poor lad! Nevertheless, this was a loss-leader defence to any legal snake oil salesman's real flim-flam mind and Boyle knew it. What the attorney was blind to was what his client had been telling the defence psychiatrists was completely at odds with what Dahmer had told Park Dietz. Jeff had effectively torpedoed Boyle's ship beneath the waterline.

On 15 February 1992, the jury found Dahmer guilty of fifteen murders with which he was charged and to which he had pleaded guilty. They also found him to be sane when he committed all fifteen murders. Two days later he was sentenced to fifteen terms of life incarceration in a state prison and not a mental institution.

Just Penance

'What a man sows he will also reap.'

Galatians 6:7

After sentencing, Dahmer was taken, in chains, to the Columbia Correctional Institution (CCI) near Portage, Wisconsin; his first year he would spend in solitary confinement due to fears that other inmates might attack him. With Dahmer's consent, after twelve months in the secure housing unit (SHU), he was moved to a less secure unit, where he was assigned a two-hour daily work detail cleaning the toilet block.

After giving his lengthy confession to Detective Murphy in 1991, Dahmer had asked for a copy of the Bible. He later claimed to have converted and become a born-again Christian. His father urged Jeffrey to read creationist books from the Institute for Creation Research, then, in May 1994, Dahmer was baptised by Roy Ratcliff, a minister in the Church of Christ and a graduate of Oklahoma Christian University. Creationism is, in itself, a highly controversial subject; it is the belief that the universe and all living organisms originate from specific acts of divine creation, and in the Biblical account, rather than by natural processes such as evolution.

Following his baptism, Ratcliffe visited with the now 'converted' Dahmer on a weekly basis up until November 1994. They discussed the prospect of death – a subject which Jeffrey was all too familiar with, being an expert on extinguishing life on a grand scale. At one point, Dahmer questioned whether he was sinning against God by continuing to live. Referring to his crimes in the 1994 interview with Stone Phillips on *Dateline NBC*, Dahmer had asked: 'If a person doesn't think that there is a God to be accountable to, what's the point of trying to modify your behaviour to keep it within acceptable ranges? That's how I thought anyway.'

In July 1994, Osvaldo R. Durruthy, a black cocaine addict/dealer, attacked Dahmer with a razor embedded in a toothbrush following Ratcliffe's weekly service in the prison chapel. The razor broke, leaving Dahmer only scratched. Then, on the morning of 28 November, 1994, Dahmer left his cell to go and clean the gym's lavatories and showers. With him were two other cleaners: Jesse Anderson, and Christopher Scarver Sr., both also convicted murderers. The trio were left inexplicably unsupervised for twenty minutes in the showers of the prison gym. Dahmer started cleaning the men's toilets whilst Anderson cleaned the locker room. Scarver was allocated the locker room where he says he picked up a steel bar from a dumbbell and beat Dahmer beyond recognition. He then went into the locker room and attacked Anderson. He then returned to his cell and informed a prison officer: 'God told me to do it.'

At approximately 8.10 a.m. Dahmer was found on the floor suffering from extreme head injuries. He had been bludgeoned about the head and face with the twenty-inch metal bar. His head had also been smashed against the wall in the attack. Barely alive, he was rushed to a nearby hospital only to be pronounced dead one hour later. Anderson died two days later.

Scarver told the warden that he had attacked both men – targeting Dahmer first. 'He didn't yell or make any noise when I attacked him,' said Scarver. He was adamant he had not planned the attacks in advance, yet he couldn't explain how the concealed metal bar had found its way into his possession. On 15 May, 1995, Scarver was sentenced to two additional life terms for the killings of Dahmer and Anderson.

Upon learning of Jeffrey's death, his mother Joyce responded angrily to the media: 'Now is everybody happy? Now that he's been bludgeoned to death, is that good enough for everyone?' The thoughts of the families of Dahmer's victims were mixed although, not surprisingly, most seemed pleased. District Attorney E. Michael McCann, an anti-death penalty advocate, cautioned against turning Scarver into a folk hero, noting that Dahmer's death was still murder.

Scarver – who is said to be schizophrenic – later claimed that he was revolted by Dahmer's crimes and the fact that he had been openly unrepentant. Scarver claimed that Dahmer taunted prison employees and fellow inmates by shaping his prison food into imitations of severed limbs, complete with ketchup to simulate blood spattering. He also claimed that prison staff, knowing of Scarver's hatred of Dahmer, had deliberately left the three men unsupervised so that he could be killed. It's true that Dahmer was so disliked by other inmates that he required a personal prison officer escort of at least one guard whenever he was out of his cell to prevent other cons from attacking him.

Jeffrey Dahmer was cremated. His ashes were split between Joyce and Lionel.

In conclusion: what made
Jeffrey Dahmer?

There have been criminologists and writers who draw distinct parallels between Dahmer and the British serial killer Dennis Andrew Nilsen, The Muswell Hill Murderer (1945-2018). Brian Masters, the biographer of Dennis 'Des' Nilsen, had advanced comparisons between Dahmer and Nilsen's murders. In his biography of Nilsen, titled *Killing for Company*, he claims that Nilsen murdered in order to stop his lovers leaving him and claims that Dahmer had similar motivation. But Colin Wilson disagrees in *Murder Casebook* Vol. 8 Part 120, saying that 'this is an unlikely explanation of his [The Milwaukee Cannibal's] crimes.'

Between 1978 and 1982, Nilsen is known to have killed a minimum of twelve men and boys, and to have attempted to kill seven others. Very much like Dahmer – and, in some respects, John Wayne Gacy – the majority of Nilsen's victims were gay men, and some were homeless too. With all three serial killers, the victims were lured to their homes using guile – typically the offer of alcohol, money or shelter. Nilsen lived at two different London addresses and once the victims were lured back to his flat, they were usually given food, the offer of a place to stay, then strangled – typically with a ligature – either to death or until they had become unconscious. If the victim had been strangled into unconsciousness, Nilsen then drowned him in his bathtub, his sink or a bucket of water before observing a ritual in which he bathed, clothed and retained the bodies inside his residence for several weeks or, occasionally months before he dismembered them. The corpses of each victim killed between 1978 and 1981 at Nilsen's first flat in Cricklewood were disposed of by burning on a bonfire. Prior to dissection, he removed their internal organs, which he disposed of either beside the fence running along the garden, or close to Gladstone Park. The young men killed in 1982 and 1983 at his Muswell Hill residence were retained at his flat, with their flesh and smaller bones flushed down the lavatory. Nilsen, like Dahmer, admitted to engaging in masturbation as he viewed the nude bodies of several of his victims, and that he engaged in sexual acts with six of them. But he was adamant he had never penetrated any of them post-mortem.

At first glance, the MOs of Dahmer and Nilsen seem very much the same; both being human flesh eaters, they were both necrophiles and used similar methods of trawling for victims and enticing them to their homes – but here the similarities end.

As awful as this may seem, there was an almost banal post-mortem reverence in the way Nilsen treated all of his prey – a respect for their bodies in an upside-down sort of way – while Dahmer treated the dead bodies of his victims like so much trash. And, of course, Dennis Nilsen didn't 'experiment' with his victims like a Nazi concentration camp doctor. So, I have come to believe that while Nilsen *did* 'kill for company' – because he kept many of the bodies around him for considerable periods of time before disposing of them – Dahmer was the polar opposite: he killed, tortured and played with his helpless prey like a cat does with terrified mice.

Many sado-sexual serial killers, back someplace in their early narratives, begin to experiment and enjoy the torturing and killing of helpless animals before they metamorphose into the killers of humans. Yet we find none of this animal cruelty with Dahmer or Nilsen; quite possibly because they were gay and of more gentle leanings in this regard. On the contrary, Dahmer loved animals and small creatures even as a morbid fascination manifested as to how they worked early in his life. I wonder how Dahmer might have felt if he had asked the same question of himself, as Dr Alice Miller might have suggested to him by psychoanalysing himself?

Nearest to Dahmer, psychologically speaking, might be Jerome 'Jerry' Brudos the Oregon sex killer (1939-2006). In the late 1960s he kidnapped girls and took them to his basement garage. He suspended them from a beam, violated them and mutilated the corpses, which he often kept around for a few days before disposing of them. He kept the foot of his first victim in the refrigerator for a few days before reluctantly getting rid of it.

If we take Dahmer's life in the round; if we were to consider this man from a child through to the end of his days at the hands of Christopher Scarver – without wandering into the realms of zombies – Jeffrey seems more dead in soul than alive. He cut a lonely figure, did he not?

He had a mentally dysfunctional mother and a strict, semi-absent and devoutly religious father. Lionel was very quick to consider that genetics might well have played no small part in his son metamorphosing into a monster. Lionel has also said that he believed homosexuality to be a sin against God and that he would have thrown Jeffrey out of the house had he learned of his sexuality at the time.

We also now know that just before he entered his teens, Dahmer had only a few meaningful friends and had started to exist in a fantasy world of his own, ambling around in the deep woods with his only companion being his dog Frisky. His home was increasingly becoming a place of unhappiness with his parents always squabbling and even sometimes coming to blows. Can one imagine what it must have felt like to him? I think most of us, if we were to put ourselves into his shoes, might also have felt pretty dejected, don't you?

In cases of juvenile isolation, bizarre fantasies and antisocial inventions are seeded as the mind becomes more introverted. With Dahmer we certainly see an interest in the occult and the tinkering with Satanism. I have interviewed several serial killers who, during their very early years, went off into their own private worlds to fantasise. Kenneth Bianchi was indeed one of them, with his so-called imaginary, invisible friend 'Little Stevie'.

As a teen, Dahmer was psychologically trapped between a rock and a hard place. He was already an alcoholic – his mind befuddled with drink, his schooling was going downhill, and he was eventually left alone to fend for himself in a house set deep in the woods. His simmering anger and frustration grew as the days passed. With no way of releasing the pressure he found himself fantasising about taking his frustrations out on the jogger who passed by his home on an almost daily basis. It was only fate that meant that this jogger went unharmed

Perhaps Jeff Dahmer can also give us some form of clue as to how he thought and what he believed, when we understand that he never apportioned any blame for what he'd done to his parents. Quite the opposite: he blamed himself. He recognised that he was starting to despise what he was becoming. This self-attributed blame mindset is very unusual amongst serial murderers and rapists. Most will try and apportion blame for their crimes onto someone else, the system, God, their parents or even their victims.

Another thing we ought to consider is this. Jeffrey Dahmer was a non-communicator. He was barely able to communicate effectively even with his mother and father let alone with the few friends he did have, many of whom regarded him as an object of ridicule to use for their own amusement. To them, Jeff was this lanky, tow-headed kid, who couldn't even get a decent date, let alone a girlfriend. I believe that 'doing a Dahmer' was his way of trying to get some form of recognition – even while his peers laughed behind his back – just at the time when his parents were petitioning for a divorce.

Regarding the failed attack on the jogger, I do not, for one moment, believe Dahmer's claim: that he only intended to knock the man out and use his unconscious body for sex. It's a ridiculous claim because the man would have come to, gone straight to the police, and probably have been able to identify his attacker. A few door-to-door enquiries would have put Jeffrey behind bars from the get-go. Dahmer identified his victim, stalked the guy and waited for him to jog past. And when the jogger failed to show up he must he been wild. But, of course, Jeffrey also claimed that he didn't mean to kill his first victims Stephen Hicks or Stephen Tuomi. In both cases, Dahmer claimed he'd woken up and 'oh, dear, me, they were both battered to death.'

Had he not become subsumed by a dependence on alcohol, Dahmer *might* just have become an 'achiever', like his father. The now-executed Connecticut serial killer, Michael Ross, once told me during an interview:

> 'Chris, I wish I could turn the clock back, but if I did I would be in the same fuckin' place as I was before. I always felt like a spider trying to crawl up a pane of glass and every time I got to the top I fell down again. Ya know, I'm not afraid of dying. I just don't want to be around when it happens.'

I think that Jeffrey Dahmer felt exactly the same way as Michael. There was no way back after he had killed Stephen Hicks. He screwed up his college education, and he could not even find his way in the army. He claimed that he loved his grandmother who pitied him, took him in to try and help reform him. And how did he repay her? He brought young men back to her beautiful, spick and span home, drugged them, raped them, killed and butchered them literally right under the old dear's nose.

So, by his later twenties he was a dropout, emotionally dead inside, a scruffy, unkempt nobody who eventually found a menial labouring job in a chocolate factory. He had been virtually alone in the world for more than ten years. Alcoholism, insecurity, lack of self-esteem, and an overwhelming craving to rape, mutilate and cannibalise, combined to turn him into one of the world's most heinous serial killers.

One cannot begin to imagine what we do *not* know about what Dahmer's victims went through: the terror, the pain, the suffering and the agonies. We can't hear their muffled screams, their desperate pleas for mercy, all falling on deaf ears, before death mercifully superseded. Without appearing to seem obtuse, the using of an electric drill to bore a hole into a drugged, semi-conscious lad's skull, to inject acid or boiling water, in a determined effort try to turn the youth into a servile, compliant zombie, is not something we come across very much these days, is it? And if that does not classify the offender as a sadist, I don't know what does. Heaven only knows what sheer hell fourteen-year-old Konerak Sinthasomphone went through, after having escaped only to be brought back by police to Dahmer's apartment of horrors. Anger would have exploded from 'The Milwaukee Cannibal', just as it did when police finally arrested him.

There will be a few forensic psychiatrists and psychologists who will vehemently disagree with me when I state that Jeffrey Dahmer was a stone-cold, sado-sexual psychopath. They will say that Jeffrey was insane, as some of the doctors at his trial argued. To prove insanity in the legal sense it is for the accused to prove that he, or she, did not know the difference between right and wrong. But Dahmer knew exactly what he was up to, went to great lengths to cover his tracks, did he not? He was well able to lie to police and to the court in previous hearings with his sackcloth and ashes bullshit that worked time and again.

Of course he was a psychopath for he had no conscience at all. Not once did he exhibit one iota of remorse for the terrible suffering he caused to not only his victims, but to their next-of-kin or friends. He was without morals and integrity. I have described his ilk before: cowards at heart; society's bottom-feeders; human scum, who crawl around unseen in our world, to prey upon the weak, vulnerable and gullible.

What perhaps is more offensive were the tactics used by Dahmer's defence team in trying to get their client off the hook, so-to-speak, in trying to spoon-feed the jury a whole pile of psycho-babble. But this is nothing new. The defence team hired shrinks – at the American taxpayers' expense – in an effort to mitigate this beast's carnage, to get him into some mental institution where he would have received far better treatment and care than he'd ever offered his prey. And there would have been the outside chance that Dahmer would have, once again, conned the psychiatrists and one day found himself a free man. Fortunately the psychiatrists employed by Dahmer's attorney could not even agree with each other, so that's nothing new either!

Well, I guess that's our psycho-travelogue pretty much reaching its end. There may be a few readers who will say 'So, what? Fuck him. He deserved all he got.' However, in dealing with Dahmer as I have striven to achieve, I leave you with a combo of the immortal words of Theodore 'Ted' Robert Bundy:

'Society wants to believe it can identify evil people, or bad or harmful people, but it's not practical. There are no stereotypes. We serial killers are your sons, we are your husbands, we are everywhere, and there will more of your children dead tomorrow. I am the most cold-hearted son of a bitch you will ever meet, so where do you think you are going?'

Sweet dreams and no nightmares please.

Appendix

Full details (by victim) of the Criminal Complaints brought against Dahmer at trial:

VICTIM JAMES DOXTATOR, DOB: 3/1/73

1) Upon the statement of the defendant, which statement is against his (the defendant's) penal interest that in January of 1988 he met a young male he thought was Hispanic who was waiting for a bus in front of the 219 Club on 2nd Street in the City and County of Milwaukee, State of Wisconsin; he (the defendant) approached him and asked him if he would like to make some money by posing in the nude, viewing videos, and having a drink at his (the defendant's) residence; at this time he (the defendant) lived at 2357 South 57th Street in the City of West Allis, County of Milwaukee, State of Wisconsin; the two of them went to that location by bus and they had sex and then he gave the young male a drink with sleeping potion and after he passed out killed him by strangling him; he dismembered him and smashed the bones with a sledgehammer and disposed of them; he did not keep any

portion of this individual; further he remembers that the young male told him that he lived with his mother in the vicinity of 10th and National; he further recalls that the young male had two scars close to each of his (the young male's) nipples that were approximately the circumference of a cigarette; the defendant viewed a copy of a booking photo of James E. Doxtater, DOB: 3/1/73, that had been taken on September 23, 1987 and indicated that he was 75% sure that this was the male that he met by the bus stop although he remembered him as looking somewhat older and heavier.

2) Upon the statement of Debra Vega, an adult citizen, that she (Vega) in January of 1988 lived at 1010 East Pierce in the City and County of Milwaukee, State of Wisconsin and that her son is James E. Doxtator, DOB: 3/1/73; she reported her son missing on January 18, 1988 and has never seen him since or been contacted by him since; further her son had two small scars in the area of his nipples that looked like cigarette burns; also that her home in 1988 at 1010 East Pierce was approximately one block from 10th and National; also that her son was a Native American.

VICTIM RICHARD GUERRERO, DOB: 12/12/65
1) Upon the further statement of the defendant, that in approximately March of 1988 he (the defendant) met a Hispanic male in the Phoenix Bar located on 2nd Street near the 219 Club in the City and County of Milwaukee, State of Wisconsin; he (the defendant) asked this man to come to his residence which at that time was his grandmother's house located at 2357 South 57th Street

in the City of West Allis, County of Milwaukee, State of Wisconsin; he asked the man to come to look at videos and take photos or engage in sex and the man came with him; they had oral sex at the house and then he drugged the man; while the man was drugged he killed him and dismembered the body and disposed of it completely without keeping any parts; he recalls that he later saw in the personal section of a local newspaper a photo of this victim and a report that he was missing; further the defendant viewed a photograph from the January 7, 1989 Milwaukee Journal of Richard Guerrero, DOB: 12-12-65, and identified this as the person he killed in this incident.

2) Upon the statement of Pablo Guerrero, an adult citizen, that he (Guerrero) is the father of Richard Guerrero and that he has not seen his son since mid-March, 1988; at that time he (Pablo Guerrero) reported his son as missing to the Milwaukee Police Department; further that advertisements with his son's picture were placed in local newspapers indicating that his son was missing.

VICTIM ANTHONY SEARS, DOB: 1/28/65

1) Upon the further statement of the defendant, that he met Anthony Sears (whom he identified in a photograph) at a club called LaCage; that a friend of Anthony Sears drove him (the defendant) and Anthony Sears to the area of his (the defendant's) grandmother's house in the City of West Allis, County of Milwaukee, State of Wisconsin; that his grandmother's house is 2357 South 57th Street; that after they arrived at that residence, they had sex and he gave Anthony Sears a drink with sleeping pills in it; that he strangled him and dismembered the body; that he kept

Anthony Sears's head and boiled it to remove the skin; further, that he kept the skull and painted it.

2) Upon the statement of Jeffrey Connor, an adult citizen, that he (Connor) was with Anthony Sears on the evening of March 25th, 1989 and on that evening they were at a bar on 6th and National; they closed the bar and that Anthony Sears had met a white male named Jeff who said that he was here from Chicago and was visiting his grandmother who lived at 56th and Lincoln; that he (Connor) then gave Jeff and Anthony Sears a ride to the vicinity of 56th and Lincoln where they (Jeff and Sears) got out of the car and walked southbound.

3) Upon complainant's personal knowledge of addresses in Milwaukee County and that the intersection of 56th and Lincoln is north of and in close proximity to the address 2357 South 57th Street in the City of West Allis.

4) Upon the statement of Dr. Jeffrey Jentzen, Milwaukee County Medical Examiner, that during the early morning hours of July 23rd, 1991 he (Jentzen) with Milwaukee police officers and other members of the County of Milwaukee Medical Examiner's Office was present at 924 North 25th Street in the City and County of Milwaukee, State of Wisconsin in Apartment 213; that he was present at that location when seven human skulls (three of which were painted) four human heads, and numerous other body parts were recovered; that all the human remains recovered were transported to the Milwaukee County Medical Examiner's Office.

5) Upon the statement of Dr. L.T. Johnson, a Forensic Odontologist, that he (Johnson) made a comparison of the painted human skulls recovered from 924 North 25th Street in the City and County of Milwaukee, State of Wisconsin during the early morning hours of July 23rd, 1991 with known dental records of Anthony Sears and determined that one of the painted skulls is that of Anthony Sears.

VICTIM RAYMOND SMITH A/K/A RICKY BEEKS, DOB: 8/10/57

1) Upon the further statement of the defendant that approximately two months after he (the defendant) moved into Apartment 213 at 924 North 25th Street in the City and County of Milwaukee, State of Wisconsin he met a black male at the 219 Club and offered him money to be photographed and have a drink and watch videos; that the man agreed and came with him (the defendant) to 924 North 25th Street, Apartment 213; that at that location he (the defendant) gave the man a drink which was drugged and the man fell asleep; that he (the defendant) then strangled the man and removed the man's clothing and had oral sex with him; further, that he dismembered the body but kept the skull and later painted it further, that he (the defendant) identified photographs of Raymond Lamont Smith as being photographs of the man to whom he had done this.

2) Upon the further statement of Dr. L.T. Johnson that he (Johnson) examined the painted skulls recovered at 924 North 25th Street in the City and County of Milwaukee,

State of Wisconsin during the early morning hours of July 23rd, 1991 with known dental records of Raymond Lamont Smith and determined that one of the aforementioned skulls is that of Raymond Smith.

3) Upon your complainant's personal observation of a copy of the defendant's rental application for the living premises at 924 North 25th Street, Apartment 213; that the aforementioned rental agreement has an initial lease date of May 13th, 1990.

VICTIM EDWARD SMITH, DOB: 8/2/62

1) Upon the further statement of the defendant, that during the Summer of 1990, approximately in July, he met a person whom he identified through a photograph as Edward W. Smith, DOB: 8-2-62, at the Phoenix Bar on 2nd Street in Milwaukee and offered him money for sex and to pose for pictures; they took a cab to his (the defendant's) apartment at 924 North 25th Street in the City and county of Milwaukee, State of Wisconsin; they had oral sex and he gave Smith a drink which contained sleeping pills and then strangled him; he dismembered Smith and took four or five photos of him; he completely disposed of Edward Smith's body by placing it in garbage bags and at a later time he also got rid of the photos of Edward Smith; he further recalls that Smith wore a headband like an Arab.

2) Upon the statement of Carolyn Smith, an adult citizen, that she (Carolyn Smith) is the sister of Edward W. Smith and that she has had no contact with him since June 23,

1990 further that her brother was called "the Sheik" because he frequently wore a turban-like wrap on his head.

VICTIM ERNEST MILLER, DOB: 5/5/67

1) Upon the statement of Vivian Miller, an adult citizen, that she (Miller) is the aunt of Ernest Miller and that on September 1st, 1990 Ernest Miller came from his home in Chicago to Milwaukee to visit for the Labor Day weekend and that he left her home during the early morning hours of September 3rd, 1990 and she has not seen him or heard from him since.

2) Upon the further statement of the defendant that during the summer of 1990 he met a black male (whom he identified through a photograph of Ernest Miller as being Ernest Miller) in front of a book store in the 800 block of North 27th Street in the City and County of Milwaukee, State of Wisconsin and that he offered the man money to return to his (the defendant's) apartment at 924 North 25th Street in the City and County of Milwaukee, State of Wisconsin; that when they returned to his apartment they had sex and then he (the defendant) drugged Ernest Miller and killed him by cutting his throat: further, that after taking photos of him, he dismembered the body and disposed of the flesh except for the biceps which he kept in the freezer; he also kept the skull which he painted after the skin was removed, and he kept the skeleton which he bleached.

3) Upon the further statement of Dr. L.T. Johnson that he (Johnson) has compared the painted skulls recovered

on July 23rd, 1991 from the defendant's apartment at 924 North 25th Street in the City and County of Milwaukee, State of Wisconsin with known dental records of Ernest Miller and determined that one of the aforementioned painted skulls is that of Ernest Miller.

VICTIM DAVID C. THOMAS, DOB: 12/21/67

1) Upon the further statement of the defendant that he in the Autumn of 1990 met a black male in the vicinity of 2nd and Wisconsin in the City and County of Milwaukee, State of Wisconsin and offered the man money to come to his apartment at 924 North 25th Street; when they got to his apartment they drank and talked but he had no sex with this man because the man wasn't his type; that he gave the man a drink with a sleeping potion in it and killed him even though he did not want to have sex with him because he thought the man would wake up and be angry; that he dismembered the body but did not keep any of the body parts because the man wasn't his type; further, that he photographed the man while he was in the process of dismembering him.

2) Upon the statement of Chandra Beanland, an adult citizen, that she (Beanland) is the girlfriend of David C. Thomas and that she reported him missing on September 24th, 1990 to the Milwaukee Police Department.

3) Upon the statement of Brian O'Keefe, a City of Milwaukee Police Detective, that he (O'Keefe) contacted the family of David C. Thomas in the course of this investigation and specifically spoke with Leslie Thomas

who identified herself as David C. Thomas's sister and that he (O'Keefe) showed Leslie Thomas the facial portion of the photograph which the defendant identified as having been taken during the course of dismembering David Thomas; further, that the facial portion showed no injuries at the time it was shown to Leslie Thomas and that Leslie Thomas identified the person in the photograph as being her brother, David Thomas; that the Thomas family supplied a photograph of David Thomas sleeping which they had; further that the face in this family photograph appeared to him (O'Keefe) to depict the same individual as in the photograph the defendant had taken while dismembering this victim.

VICTIM CURTIS STRAUGHTER, DOB: 4/16/73

1) Upon the statement of Katherine Straughter, an adult citizen, that she (Straughter) is the grandmother of Curtis Straughter and that she last saw her grandson on February 18th, 1991.

2) Upon the further statement of the defendant that in February of 1991 he observed Curtis Straughter (whom he identified through a photograph) waiting for a bus by Marquette University and offered him money to come back to his apartment at 924 North 25th Street in the City and County of Milwaukee, State of Wisconsin; that Straughter did accompany him back and at the apartment he (the defendant) gave Curtis Straughter a drugged drink and had oral sex with him; the defendant then strangled him with a strap and dismembered the body; he also took photos and kept the man's skull.

3) Upon the further statement of Dr. L.T. Johnson that he (Johnson) compared the unpainted skulls recovered from the defendant's apartment with known dental records of Curtis Straughter and determined that one of the unpainted skulls was that of Curtis Straughter.

VICTIM ERROL LINDSEY, DOB: 3/3/72

1) Upon the statement of Yahuna Barkley, an adult citizen, that she (Barkley) is the sister of Errol Lindsey and that she last saw him on April 7th, 1991 when he went to the store and that she has not seen him since that time.

2) Upon the further statement of the defendant that in the Spring of 1991 he met Errol Lindsey (whom he identified by photograph) on the corner of 27th and Kilbourn in the City and County of Milwaukee, State of Wisconsin and that he offered Errol Lindsey money to return with him (the defendant) to his apartment at 924 North 25th Street in the City and County of Milwaukee, State of Wisconsin; that after they returned to his apartment he gave Lindsey a drugged drink and after he fell asleep he strangled Lindsey and then had oral sex with him; he then dismembered the body and saved the skull.

3) Upon the further statement of Dr. L.T. Johnson that he (Johnson) compared the unpainted skulls recovered from the defendant's apartment on July 23rd, 1991 with known dental records of Errol Lindsey and determined that one of the unpainted skulls is that of Errol Lindsey.

VICTIM TONY ANTHONY HUGHES, DOB: 8/26/59

1) Upon the further statement of the defendant that in May of 1991 he met Tony Anthony Hughes (whom he identified through a photograph) who was deaf and mute in front of the 219 Bar on Second Street in the City and County of Milwaukee, State of Wisconsin; that he communicated with Hughes by writing and it appeared that Hughes could read lips; that he offered Hughes $50 to come to his (the defendant's) apartment at 924 North 25th Street in the City and County and Milwaukee, State of Wisconsin to take photos and view videos; further, that he gave Hughes a drink with a sleeping potion and then killed him and dismembered his body and kept his skull.

2) Upon the further statement of Dr. L.T. Johnson that he (Johnson) has compared the unpainted skulls found in the apartment of the defendant with known dental records of Tony Hughes and determined that one of the unpainted skulls is that of Tony Hughes.

3) Upon the statement of Shirley Hughes, an adult citizen, that she (Hughes) is the mother of Tony Hughes and that Tony Hughes came to Milwaukee from Madison during the late afternoon or evening of May 24th, 1991 and that she has not seen him since and further that her son, Tony Hughes, is deaf and mute.

VICTIM KONERAK SINTHASOMPHONE, DOB: 12/2/76

1) Upon the statement of Sounthone Sinthasomphone, an adult resident, that he is the father of Konerak

Sinthasomphone who was 14 years of age and that during the afternoon of May 26th, 1991 his son left home and did not return and he has not seen him since.

2) Upon the further statement of the defendant that he (the defendant) in late May of 1991 met a young Oriental male (whom he identified by photograph as Konerak Sinthasomphone) in front of Grand Avenue Mall in Milwaukee and that they went back to his (the defendant's) apartment at 924 North 25th Street in the City and County of Milwaukee, State of Wisconsin; that Sinthasomphone posed for two photographs while he was alive and that he (the defendant) gave Sinthasomphone a drink laced with a sleeping potion and that they then watched videos and while they were watching videos, Sinthasomphone passed out; that he (the defendant) then had oral sex with Sinthasomphone and then he (the defendant) went to a bar to get some beer because he had run out; that while he was walking back from the bar located on 27th just North of Kilbourn, he saw Sinthasomphone staggering down the street and he (the defendant) went up to Sinthasomphone and then the police stopped him; that he told the police that he was a friend of this individual and that the individual had gotten drunk and done this before; that the police escorted them back to his (the defendant's) apartment and he told the police he would take care of Sinthasomphone because he was his friend; that they went into the apartment and after the police left, he killed Sinthasomphone by strangling him and then had oral sex with him and then he took

more photographs and dismembered the body and kept the skull.

3) Upon the further statement of Dr. L.T. Johnson that he (Johnson) compared the unpainted skulls recovered from the apartment at 924 North 25th Street with known dental records of Konerak Sinthasomphone and determined that one of the skulls which was recovered from that location is that of Konerak Sinthasomphone.

VICTIM MATT TURNER A/K/A DONALD MONTRELL, DOB: 7/3/70

1) Upon the further statement of the defendant that on June 30th, 1991 after the Gay Pride Parade in Chicago, he met a black male at the Chicago Bus Station and offered him money to pose nude and also view videos at his apartment back in Milwaukee: he (the defendant), with this black male, returned to Milwaukee on a Greyhound Bus and then took a City Vet cab to his (the defendant's) residence in Apartment 213 at 924 North 25th Street, in the City and County of Milwaukee, State of Wisconsin; he (the defendant) gave the black male something to drink which had been drugged and the man passed out and he (the defendant) used a strap to strangle the man and then dismembered him and kept his head and put it in the freezer in his apartment and placed his body in a 57 gallon barrel that he had in his residence; further that he (the defendant) looked at a photograph supplied by the Chicago Police Department of Matt Turner a/k/a Donald Montrell and indicated that he thought this was the person that he had killed in this incident.

VICTIM JEREMIAH WEINBERGER, DOB: 9/29/67

1) Upon the further statement of the defendant that on or about July 5th, 1991 he met a Puerto Rican male at Carol's Gay Bar on Wells Street in Chicago and that he offered the man money to come with him to Milwaukee to pose for him and to view videos: they took a Greyhound Bus from Chicago to Milwaukee and then took a cab to the defendant's apartment at 924 North 25th Street in the City and County of Milwaukee, State of Wisconsin; this man stayed with him for two days and on the first day they had oral sex and on the second day the man indicated that he wanted to leave and he (the defendant) didn't want the man to leave so he gave him a drink with a sleeping potion in it and strangled him manually and then took photos of him and dismembered the body; he then took more photos and kept the man's head in the freezer and body in the 57 gallon drum; he (the defendant) looked at a photo supplied by the Chicago Police Department of Jeremiah Weinberger and indicated that this was the man that he had killed in this incident.

2) Upon the statement of Dr. L.T. Johnson that he (Johnson) at the Milwaukee County Medical Examiner's Office compared one of the human heads recovered from the freezer at 924 North 25th Street with known dental records of Jeremiah Weinberger and determined that the severed human head that he examined in comparison with those records was the head of Jeremiah Weinberger.

VICTIM OLIVER LACY, DOB: 6/23/67

1) Upon the further statement of the defendant that on or about July 15th, 1991 he met a black male on 27th

Street between State and Kilbourn in Milwaukee and that the man stated he was going to his cousin's house; he invited the man to his residence to pose for photos and the man agreed to come and model; when they got to the residence at 924 North 25th Street in the City and County of Milwaukee, State of Wisconsin, they removed their clothes and did body rubs and he gave the man a drink which had sleeping potion in it; when the man fell asleep, he strangled him and then had anal sex with him after death; he dismembered the body and placed the man's head in the bottom of the refrigerator in a box and kept the man's heart in the freezer to eat later; he also kept the man's body in the freezer; he kept the man's identification which identified the man as Oliver Lacy, date of birth 6/23/67.

VICTIM JOSEPH BRADEHOFT, DOB: 1/24/66

1) Upon the further statement of the defendant that on or about July 19th, 1991 he met a white male on Wisconsin Avenue near Marquette University; the man was waiting for a bus and had a six pack under his arm; he (the defendant) got off a bus at that location and approached the man and offered him money to pose and view videos and the man agreed; they returned to the defendant's residence at 924 North 25th Street in the City and County of Milwaukee, State of Wisconsin; they had oral sex and then he gave the man a drink with a sleeping potion in it and then strangled him with a strap while he slept; he dismembered this man and put his head in the freezer and his body in the same blue 57 gallon barrel where he had placed the bodies of the black male and the Puerto Rican male; he kept this

man's identification card which identified him as Joseph Bradehoft, date of birth 1/24/66.

Evidence submitted at Dahmer's trial:

A: Box containing Explorer bushwhacker, model 21-166, knife with black leather sheath, (MWPD INV #1337835, Items #1 and #2)

B: Wooden spoon, (MWPD INV #1337860, Item #1)

C: Disston handsaw with 6 1/2" blade, (MWPD INV #1337860, Item #2)

D: Handsaw with black plastic handle and 12" blade, (MWPD INV #1337860, Item #5)

E: 15 ¾" saw blade, (MWPD INV #1337860, Item #6)

F: 13 ¼" saw blade, (MWPD INV #1337860, Item #7)

G: 12 ¼" saw blade, (MWPD INV #1337860, Item #8)

H: Black 12 ¼" saw blade, (MWPD INV #1337960, Item #9)

I: Knife with white plastic handle, (MWPD INV #1337855, Item #2)

J: Ekco knife with 4 1/8" blade, (MWPD INV #1337855, Item #3)

K: Sheffield knife with 3" blade, (MWPD INV #1337855, Item #4)

L: Oral B toothbrush, (MWPD INV #1337855, Item #5)

M: Electric drill, Sears Craftsman, 3/8", (MWPD INV #1337855, Item #9)

N: Myoda lap-top computer, model LT3500, ser/35002853, (MWPD INV #1337824, Item #9)

O: Software, Central Point software kit, (MWPD INV #1337872, Item #2)

P: User's manual for lap-top computer, model LT3500, (MWPD INV #1337872, Item #3)

Q: Computer guide – Microsoft Learning DOS, (MWPD INV #1337872, Item #4

R: Hypodermic needle, (MWPD INV #1337822, Item #2)

S: Paper bag contg filter and vacuumed debris from carpet, (MWPD INV #1338728, Item #2)

T: Paper bag contg filter and vacuumed residue from aluminium pot, (MWPD INV #1338728, Item #2)

U: Paper bag contg filter and vacuumed residue from file cabinet, (MWPD INV #1338728, Item #3)

V: Floor tiles, 2 pieces, (MWPD INV #1338728, Item #4)

W: Sample of stained fabric from beneath cushions of couch, (MWPD INV #1338730, Item #1)

X: Sample of stained fabric from cushion of couch, (MWPD INV #1338730, Item #2)

Y: Sample of unstained fabric from beneath cushions of couch, (MWPD INV #1338730, Item #3)

Z: Sample of unstained fabric from couch, (MWPD INV #1338730, Item #4)

AA: Sample of stained fabric from beneath chair cushion, (MWPD INV #1338730, Item #5)

AB: Sample of unstained fabric from beneath chair cushion, (MWPF INV #1338731, Item #1)

AC: Sample of stained fabric from chair, (MWPD INV #1338731, Item #2)

AD: Sample of stained fabric from chair, (MWPD INV #1338731, Item #3)

AE: Sample of unstained fabric from chair, (MWPD INV #1338731, Item #4)

AF: Collection bag from Mighty-Mini shop vac (MWPD INV #1338731, Item #5)

AG: Filter from Mighty-Mini shop vac (MWPD INV #1338731, Item #6)

AH: Paper bag contg scrapings of dried material on stove top, (MWPD INV #1338732, Item #1)

AI: Paper bag contg scrapings of dried material inside dishpan, (MWPD INV #1338732, Item #2)

AJ: Small drill bit, MWPD INV #1338732, Item #3)

AK: Sample of mattress pad, unstained, (MWPD INV #1338732, Item #4)

AL: Sample of mattress pad, stained, (MWPD INV #1338732, Item #5)

AM: Pillowcase, black cloth, bloodstained, (MWPD INV #133872, Item 6)

AN: Sample of cloth from pillow, stained, (MWPD INV #1338733, Item #1)

AO: Sample of cloth from pillow, unstained, (MWPD INV #1338733, Item #2)

AP: Sample of sheet, unstained, (MWPD INV #1338733, Item #3)

AQ: Sample of sheet stained, (MWPD INV #1338733, Item #4)

AR: Sample of hall carpet, unstained, (MWPD INV #1338733, Item #5)

AS: Sample of hall carpet, stained, (MWPD (INV #1338733, Item #1)

AT: Sample of mattress fabric, stained, (MWPD INV #1338734, Item #1)

AU: Sample of mattress fabric, stained, (MWPD INV #1338734, Item #2)

AV: Sample of mattress fabric, unstained, (MWPD INV #1338734, Item #3)

AW: Sample of box spring fabric, stained, (MWPD INV #1338734, Item #4)

AX: Sample of box spring fabric, unstained, (MWPD INV #1338734, Item #5)

AY: Sample of bedroom carpet pad, stained, (MWPD INV #1338735, Item #1)

AZ: Sample of bedroom carpet pad, stained, (MWPD INV #1338735, Item #2)

BA: Sample of bedroom carpet pad, unstained, (MWPD INV #1338735, Item #3)

BB: Sample of bedroom carpet pad, stained, (MWPD INV #13385737, Item #4)

BC: Sample of bedroom carpet, stained, (MWPD INV #1338735, Item #5)

BD: Sample of bedroom carpet, stained, (MWPD INV #1338736, Item #1)

BE: Sample of bedroom carpet, unstained. (MWPD INV #1338736, Item #2)

BF: Sample of bedroom carpet, stained, (MWPD INV #1338736, Item #3)

BG: Sample of bedroom carpet, stained, (MWPD INV #1338736. Item #4)

BH: Sample of living room carpet, stained, (MWPD INV #1338736, Item #5)

BI: Sample of living room carpet pad, unstained, (MWPD INV #1338736, Item #6)

BJ: Sample of living room carpet pad, stained, (MWPD INV #1338736, Item #7)

BK: Sample of living room carpet, stained, (MWPD INV #1338736, Item #8)

BL: Sealed envelope contg oral and anal swabs and smears, saliva sample, head hair, public hair, hairs from torso, and left and right fingernail clippings from remains of Oliver Lacy at post-mortem exam, (MWPD INV #1338900, Item #1)

BM: Sealed bag contg frozen samples of lumbar margin, bone marrow and anterior 6th rib cartilage from remains of Oliver Lacy and post-mortem exam, (MWPD INV #1338900, Item 2)

BN: Sealed envelope contg oral and anal swabs and smears, saliva sample, head hair and hair from anus from remails of Joseph Bradenhoft [sic] at post-mortem exam, (MWPD INV #1338901, Item #1)

BO: Sealed bag contg frozen samples of cervical and lumbar margins and bone marrow from remains of Joseph Bradenhoft [sic] at post-mortem exam, (MWPD INV #1338091, Item #2)

BP: Sealed envelope contg oral and anal swabs and smears, laryngel swabs and smears, saliva sample and head hair from remains of Jeremiah Weinberger at post-mortem exam (MWPD INV #1338902, Item #1)

BQ: Sealed bag contg frozen cervical and lumbar margins, bone marrow and sample of skull with drill holes from remains of Jeremiah Weinberger, MWPD INV #1338902, Item #2)

BR: Sealed envelope contg upper molars and sample of skull with drill holes from remains of Konerak Sinthasomphone at post-mortem exam, (MWPD INV #1338930, Item #1)

BS: Sealed envelope contg upper molars and sample of skull with drill holes from remains of Tony Hughes at post-mortem exam, (MWPD INV #1338904, Item #1)

BT: Sealed envelope contg upper molars and sample of paint from skull of Earnest [sic] Miller at post-mortem exam, (MWPD INV #1338905, Item #1)

BU: Sealed envelope contg pubic hair standards and combings, head hair, upper molars and sample of paint from skull of remains of Anthony Sears at post-mortem exam, (MWPD INV #1338906, Item #1)

BV: Sealed envelope contg upper molars and sample of skull with drill holes from remains of Raymond Smith at post-mortem exam, (MWPD INV #1338908, Item #1)

BW: Sealed envelope contg upper molars and sample of skull with drill holes from remains of Errol Lindsey at post-mortem exam, (MWPD INV #1338908, Item #)

BX: Sealed envelope contg public hair combings and standards, and upper molars from remains of Curtis Straughter at post-mortem exam, (MWPD INV #1338914, Item #1)

BY: Sealed envelope contg head hair, oral and anal swabs and smears, and saliva sample from remains of Matt Turner at post-mortem exam, (MWPD INV #1338915, Item #1)

BZ: Sealed bag contg frozen cervical and lumbar margins, bone marrow, hair from pelvis, skin pieces and eight costal margins from remains of Matt Turner at postmortem exam, (MWPD INV #1338915, Item #2)

CA: Blood sample in glass vial, sealed in plastic bag, obtained from Jeffrey L. Dahmer, W/M, DOB: 5/21/60, (MWPD INV #1338970, Item #1)

CB: Head hair sample obtained from Jeffrey L. Dahmer, W/M, DOB: 5/21/60, (MWPD INV #1338970, Item #2)

CC: Pubic hair samples obtained from Jeffrey L. Dahmer, W/M, DOB: 5/21/60, MWPD INV #, Item #3)

CD: Polaroid photo depicting homicide victim, Jeremiah Weinberger, and right leg and foot of suspect, (MWPD INV #1339825, Item #1)

CE: Polaroid photo depicting homicide victim, Ernest Miller, and left hand and fore-arm of suspect, (MWPD INV #1339825, Item #2)

CF: Polaroid photo depicting homicide victim, David Thomas, (MWPD INV #1339825, Item #3)

CG: Black pillowcase, bloodstained, (MWPD INV #1337844, Item #5)

CH: Blood samples and controls, (MWPD INV 1337904, Item #1)

NOTES

1 *Hannibal* (2001) directed by Ridley Scott.
2 *The Jeffrey Dahmer Story: An American Nightmare* by Don M. Davies (Mass Market Paperback, 2003)
3 *The Drama of the Gifted Child* by Dr Alice Miller (Basic Books, 2008)
4 *The Guardian*, 2005 https://www.theguardian.com/society/2005/apr/20/childrensservices.books
5 *The Shrine of Jeffrey Dahmer* by Brian Masters (Hodder & Stoughton, 2020)
6 https://www.zmescience.com/science/psychology-science/children-toys-07022013/
7 https://pubmed.ncbi.nlm.nih.gov/21864144/
8 https://theconversation.com/how-young-children-understand-death-and-how-to-talk-to-them-about-it-96134?utm_source=twitter&utm_medium=twitterbutton
9 *The Shrine of Jeffrey Dahmer* by Brian Masters (Hodder & Stoughton, 2020)
10 *The Shrine of Jeffrey Dahmer* by Brian Masters (Hodder & Stoughton, 2020)

11 *The Shrine of Jeffrey Dahmer* by Brian Masters (Hodder & Stoughton, 2020)

12 https://pubs.niaaa.nih.gov/publications/arh284/213-221.htm

13 https://epublications.regis.edu/cgi/viewcontent.cgi?article=1240&context=theses

14 *The Jeffrey Dahmer Story: An American Nightmare* by Don M. Davies (Mass Market Paperback, 2003)

15 https://vault.fbi.gov/jeffrey-lionel-dahmer/jeffrey-lionel-dahmer-part-03-of-19

16 https://www.sciencedirect.com/topics/medicine-and-dentistry/necrophilia

17 *The Jeffrey Dahmer Story: An American Nightmare* by Don M. Davies (Mass Market Paperback, 2003)

18 *The Jeffrey Dahmer Story: An American Nightmare* by Don M. Davies (Mass Market Paperback, 2003)